Theories and Practices in Second Language Learning and Teaching

Theories and Practices in Second Language Learning and Teaching

초판 1쇄 인쇄　2017년 6월 20일
초판 1쇄 발행　2017년 6월 26일

지 은 이　김지현
펴 낸 이　신일희
펴 낸 곳　계명대학교 출판부
출판등록　제347-1998-1호(1970. 9. 1)
주　　소　대구광역시 달서구 달구벌대로 1095
대표전화　053-580-6233
팩　　스　053-580-6235
홈페이지　www.kmupress.com

ISBN　978-89-7585-784-3　93370　정가 21,000원

이 도서의 국립중앙도서관 출판예정도서목록(CIP)은 서지정보유통지원시스템 홈페이지(http://seoji.nl.go.kr)와 국가자료공동목록시스템(http://www.nl.go.kr/kolisnet)에서 이용하실 수 있습니다.(CIP제어번호: CIP2017014648)

Theories and Practices in Second Language Learning and Teaching

김 지 현

KEIMYUNG UNIVERSITY PRESS

PREFACE

Theories and Practices in Second Language Learning and Teaching aims to introduce current theories in second language learning and teaching, alongside historical perspectives to discuss the origins of these ideas. Furthermore, as the title anticipates, this book includes practices as well. Many of the published books in this field focus on either theory or practice. There is a good reason for this. There are a wealth of arguments and issues to be considered in discussions about second language learning and teaching; thus, including both theory and practice in one book might appear excessive. However, my experience teaching undergraduate pre-service English teachers in Korea made me realize the necessity of a book which concisely introduces teachers to the basic concepts of both theory and practice simultaneously in order to establish the elementary knowledge of second language learning and teaching. At the same time, I realized that it was not possible to cover all of the chapters in a published book within a semester, so I had to be selective in choosing which chapters I needed to teach, and inevitably some chapters were always left out. Thus, in planning this book, my priority has been to carefully select what undergraduate pre-service English teachers should know about language learning and teaching. I personally believe that using teaching techniques without an understating of the theories that inform these practices is like 'building a sandcastle' and 'a tree with no root.' Understanding the theoretical foundations of techniques enables teachers to modify the skills according to their students' needs, interests, and proficiency, which is one of the most important pedagogical skills required in the classroom. For this reason, I tried to balance theories and practices in each chapter. I also included many examples in order to bolster student understanding of the complicated concepts and ideas that inform second language learning and teaching.

This book consists of 10 chapters. Chapter 1 introduces the vital second language acquisition theories which have influenced the field of second language teaching. Chapter 2 addresses issues which lead to individual learner differences in the outcome of second language learning. Chapter 3 covers historical and current second language teaching methods to inform students' understanding of how teaching methods have been advanced. Chapters 4 to 7 focus on teaching four skills, listening, speaking, reading, and writing. Needless to say, these four skills need to be developed simultaneously. However, prior to practicing integrative skills, it is necessary to study the theoretical foundations and practical techniques for classroom instruction related to each skill. Chapter 8 covers grammar instruction. While grammar instruction was outmoded for a while, it is currently on the rise again. Chapter 9 explains how to plan a lesson with practical step-by-step tips, while Chapter 10 introduces basic principles that language teachers should know when they assess student performance and achievement.

It is my hope that this book equips pre-service teachers with the essential knowledge and insights about second language learning and teaching, thereby serving as a guide in their journey to be teachers of second language. Additionally, this book can be used as a suitable resource for educators or instructors teaching second language learning and teaching in university.

CONTENTS

PREFACE ··· 4

CH. 1
Second Language Acquisition Theories

Behaviorists' Perspectives on Language Learning ··· 17
  Perspectives on Frist Language Learning ··· 18
  Perspectives on Second Language Learning ··· 19
  Contrastive Analysis ··· 20
  Behaviorism, Contrastive Analysis, and Second Language Teaching ··· 22
  Counter Evidence to the Contrastive Analysis Hypothesis ··· 22
Innativists' Perspectives on Language Learning ··· 25
  Universal Grammar (UG) ··· 26
  UG in First Language Acquisition ··· 27
  UG in Second Language Acquisition ··· 28
  Second Language Learning Theory within UG: The Monitor Model ··· 30
    Acquisition-learning hypothesis ··· 31

Monitor hypothesis … 32
Natural order hypothesis … 33
Input hypothesis … 33
Affective filter hypothesis … 35
Critics on Krashen's view … 36
Cognitivists' Views on Language Acquisition … 38
Information Processing Models … 38
Automaticity and proceduralization through practice … 40
Restructuring … 40
Learner Languages from Cognitive Views … 43
Error analysis … 44
Input, Interaction, Output, and Attention in Second Language Acquisition … 46
Input in Language Acquisition … 47
Input for comprehension vs. acquisition … 48
Interaction in Second Language Learning … 49
Interaction hypothesis … 50
Corrective feedback in interaction … 53
Output in Second Language Learning … 58
Attention in Second Language Learning … 62
Noticing hypothesis … 63
Sociocultural Theory … 65
Zone of Proximal Development … 66
Other Regulation and Self-Regulation … 67
Chapter Concluding Remarks … 69

CH. 2

Learner Individual Differences

Motivation … 74
Language Learning Aptitude … 77
Learning Styles … 80
Personality … 83
Willingness to Communicate … 85
Learning Strategies … 86
Age … 90
Effects of Age on Second Language Learning … 91
Some empirical studies into age and second language learning … 91
Explanations for age-related phenomenon … 95
Chapter Concluding Remarks … 96

CH. 3

Teaching Methods and Approaches

Early Approaches to Language Teaching … 102
The Grammar-Translation Method … 102
The Direct Method … 103
The Audiolingual Approach … 104
More Recent Approaches to Language Teaching … 105
The Cognitive Approach … 105
The Affective-Humanistic Approach … 106
The Comprehension Approach … 107
The Communicative Approach … 107
Communicative language teaching … 108
Content-based instruction … 113
Task-based instruction … 115
Chapter Concluding Remarks … 117

CH. 4

Teaching Listening

Process of Listening Comprehension: Top-down vs. Bottom-up Processes ··· 122
Transactional and Interactional Languages ··· 124
Classroom Instruction ··· 127
Selecting Listening Materials ··· 127
Relevance ··· 127
Authenticity ··· 127
Task difficulty ··· 130
Types of text feature ··· 132
Using Three Stages of Listening ··· 132
Pre-listening stage ··· 133
While-listening stage ··· 135
Post-listening stage ··· 139
Developing Listening Strategies ··· 140
Chapter Concluding Remarks ··· 142

CH. 5

Teaching Speaking

Different Types of Speaking Events ··· 148
The Foundation of Competent Second Language Speaking ··· 149
Fluency and Accuracy ··· 150
Appropriacy ··· 150
Authenticity ··· 152
Corpus-based second language instruction ··· 153
Conversation analysis ··· 154
Classroom Instruction ··· 154
Accuracy-Oriented Tasks vs. Fluency-Oriented Tasks ··· 154

Accuracy-based activities … 155
Fluency-based activities … 158
Sample activities … 160
Balancing activities … 164
Selecting Activity … 165
Corrective Feedback in Teaching Speaking … 165
Which error to correct … 167
When to correct the errors … 168
How to correct the errors … 168
Teaching Pronunciation … 170
Chapter Concluding Remarks … 172

CH. 6

Teaching Reading

Reading Processes … 176
Intensive Reading and Extensive Reading … 177
Authenticity of Reading Materials … 179
Classroom Instruction … 182
Developing and Utilizing Learners' Background Knowledge … 182
Selecting Proper Reading Materials … 183
Using Reading Aloud in the Classroom … 184
Working on Fluent Reading … 185
Teaching Reading Strategies … 186
Implementing Three Stages of Reading … 188
Pre-reading stage … 188
While-reading stage … 189
Post-reading stage … 189
Triggering Learner Motivation … 194
Chapter Concluding Remarks … 196

CH. 7

Teaching Writing

Differences between Written and Spoken Languages ··· 200
Genres and Register ··· 201
Formal Writing and Informal Writing ··· 202
Product-Oriented vs. Process-Oriented Writing ··· 202
Coherences and Cohesion ··· 204
Classroom Instruction ··· 207
Balancing Product and Process ··· 207
Using Process-Oriented Writing to Teach Writing Process ··· 207
Using Collaborative Writing ··· 212
Making Feedback Helpful and Meaningful ··· 214
Types of Classroom Writing Activities ··· 215
Chapter Concluding Remarks ··· 220

CH. 8

Teaching Grammar

Principles for Teaching Grammar ··· 224
Deductive vs. Inductive Approaches ··· 224
Form-Meaning-Function Mapping ··· 227
Classroom Instruction ··· 230
Presentation-Practice-Production vs. Task-Based Grammar Instruction ··· 230
Presentation-practice-production (PPP) ··· 230
Task-based grammar instruction ··· 232
Characteristics of PPP vs. task-based grammar instruction ··· 234
Input-Based Grammar Instruction ··· 235
Input enhancement ··· 236
Processing instruction ··· 237

Classroom Techniques and Activities ··· 240
Chapter Concluding Remarks ··· 243

CH. 9

Planning a Lesson

Designing a Plan ··· 248
Lesson Objectives ··· 248
Activities and Procedures ··· 250
Consolidation ··· 251
Implementing the Plan ··· 252
Reflecting the Lesson ··· 253
Chapter Concluding Remarks ··· 253

CH. 10

Assessment and Testing

Types of Assessment ··· 257
Informal and Formal Assessment ··· 258
Formative and Summative Assessment ··· 259
Discrete-Point Tests and Integrative Tests ··· 259
Norm-Referenced and Criterion-Referenced Tests ··· 262
Achievement Tests ··· 263
Diagnostic Tests ··· 263
Proficiency Tests ··· 264
Placement Tests ··· 265
Principles of Assessment ··· 265
Reliability ··· 265
Validity ··· 269

Content validity ··· 269
Criterion validity ··· 270
Construct validity ··· 271
Practicality ··· 271
Authenticity ··· 272
Washback ··· 272
Alternative Assessment ··· 273
Portfolios ··· 274
Reflective Journals ··· 276
Chapter Concluding Remarks ··· 277

GLOSSARY ··· 278
BIBLIOGRAPHY ··· 290

Chapter 1

Second Language Acquisition Theories

Chapter 1.

Second Language Acquisition Theories

Second language acquisition theories describe how people learn non-primary languages and the factors that facilitate or hinder language learning. Comprehending language learning processes is essential for second and foreign language teachers since it helps them to understand learners' learning process, and this eventually enables them to provide effective instruction. This chapter will introduce five perspectives on second language acquisition theories that have been most extensively discussed and applied in language teaching.

Behaviorists' Perspectives on Language Learning

Behaviorism is one of the most influential learning theories in the 1940s and 1950s. Behaviorism attempts to explain all behaviors without reference to mental and internal processes. Rather, all mental and physical activities are explained as responses to external factors (stimulus) in the environment. Behaviorists believe that human behavior could be understood by investigating animal behavior. Thus, their claims about learning are based on investigations with animals. They maintain that behavior is both conditioned and reinforced by its own outcomes or consequences such as rewards and punishments. In other words, any human behavior followed by a reward would become reinforced and thus more likely to occur in the future. In contrast, any behavior which causes punishments would be relinquished and thus would not take place again. With sufficient repetitions of certain stimulated behaviors with reinforcement, the behavior would become a habit. In sum, they contend that human behavior is solely a result of the association of events, a response to environmental stimuli and subsequent reinforcement.

• Perspectives on First Language Learning

Behaviorists see all learning, including language learning, as the acquisition of a new behavior. The environment surrounding language learners is the most important factor in learning since they need to receive consistent stimuli and positive reinforcement (praise or successful communication) and/or punishment. In first language acquisition, children learn a language by imitating sounds and structures they hear in the environment (stimuli-response). When children imitate the language they have heard, their attempts to reproduce it receive positive reinforcement (praise or successful communication), and this could encourage them to continue to imitate and practice the sounds and patterns until they form habits of correct language use.

• Perspectives on Second Language Learning

According to behaviorists, second language learning takes place in a similar fashion. In order to learn a new language, a learner must be exposed to correct models of the language and imitate them repeatedly. Needless to say, reinforcement and/or punishment should be provided. In the examples below, the positive reinforcement ("Good") of the accurate imitation will promote the student to continue to use "Where is the book?" while the correction of inaccurate imitation ("No, say…") will stop the student from using "Where the book." Imitation, repetition, and practice with reinforcement will bring about habit formation.

Example 1.1

Teacher:	Where is the book?
Student:	Where is the book?
Teacher:	Good. Where is the pencil?

Example 1.2

Teacher:	Where is the book?
Student:	Where the book?
Teacher:	No, say 'where is the book?' Again.

As mentioned above, in behaviorisms, the key mechanism

that brings about first and second language acquisition is the same. Second language learning is seen as the development of a new set of habits. However, one thing that distinguishes second language acquisition from first language acquisition is that second language learners already have a set of first language habits. Second language learners should overcome first language habits in the process of acquiring a new language. Otherwise, first language habits would interfere with the establishment of a new set of second language habits. Behaviorists blame the lack of success in second language learning on the use of first language habits in attempting to produce and the comprehend the second language, which is called *transfer*. Transfer could have either positive or negative consequences, depending on the distance between the first language and the second language. From this framework, behaviorism is tied to the *contrastive analysis hypothesis* (CAH) since if one is to talk about replacing a set of habits, comparing the 'rules' of the two languages is necessary.

• Contrastive Analysis

In contrastive analysis (CA), the first language and the second language are compared by a structure-by-structure comparison of the sound system, morphological system, syntactic system, and even the cultural systems of two languages in order to discover similarities and differences. According to the contrastive analysis hypothesis, wherever languages are similar, there will be *positive transfer*; wherever languages are dissimilar, there will be *negative transfer*. In the former case, learners will have little difficulty because they will simply be able to use their old habits in using the second language. In contrast, in the latter case, learners will have difficulty and make errors. This type of error is called *interference errors*. Below the assumptions the contrastive analysis hypothesis is based on are summarized:

> 1. Contrastive analysis is based on a theory of language that claims that language is habit and that language learning involves the establishment of a new set of habits.
> 2. The major source of error in the production and/or reception of a second language is the native language.
> 3. One can account for errors by considering differences between the first language and the second language.
> 4. A corollary to item 3 is that the greater the differences, the more errors will occur.
> 5. What one has to do in learning a second language is learn the differences. Similarities can be safely ignored as no new learning is involved. In other words, what is dissimilar between two languages is what must be learned.
> 6. Difficulty and ease in learning is determined receptively by differences and similarities between the two languages in contrast.
>
> (Adapted from Gass & Selinker, 2008, pp. 96–97)

By discovering the similarities and differences between the languages, one can predict areas that will be either easy or difficult for learners, which is indeed the ultimate goal of contrastive analysis. Furthermore, one can determine potential errors and decide what needs to be learned and what does not need to be learned in a second language learning situation.

• Behaviorism, Contrastive Analysis, and Second Language Teaching

Based on behaviorism and the contrastive analysis hypothesis, several implications of second language teaching can be suggested. First, the role of first language in second language learning is emphasized. Specifically, the extent of the difference between the first language and the second language decides the degree of difficulty learners will feel in learning the second language. Difference is related to difficulty. Second, the difference between the first language and the second language is the primary source of errors. Thus, where the contrast between the two languages is greater, greater difficulty and, consequently, more errors can be predicted. An important goal of language teaching is to help learners avoid such interference errors. Third, repetition of correct models along with immediate and consistent corrective feedback to errors is considered the best way to stamp out errors before learners develop bad habits. Lastly, habit formation is considered the outcome of response to external stimuli rather than internal process. There is little need for learners to reflect on their learning process, so they only need to repeat what they listen to.

• Counter Evidence to the Contrastive Analysis Hypothesis

The contrastive analysis hypothesis assumes that the first language is the driving force of second language learning: learner errors could be predicted based on the analysis of the differences between first and second languages. However, a great deal of second language research (Dušková, 1984; Kellerman, 1987; Zobl, 1980) shows empirical findings against the contrastive analysis hypothesis, revealing that learners' errors cannot be explained by only first language interference.

Zobl (1980), for instance, in data from French speakers learning English and English speakers learning French, found inconsistencies in actual error production. In French, object pronoun precedes the verb, and in English, object pronouns follow the verb as in the example below:

Je les vois. (I them see)
I see them.

Based on the contrastive analysis hypothesis, we can easily predict that French speakers would make sentences like **I them see*, following French word order while English speakers would produce a sentence like **Je vois les*, using the English word order. However, the following data emerged in learner data:

By French learners of English
I see them. (produced)
*I them see. (not produced)

By English learners of French
*Je voiselle.
(I see her.)
*Le chien a mange les.
(The dog has eaten them.)

French learners of English never proposed the object

pronoun. In other words, they did not follow the French word order. Rather, they correctly followed the English word order, which in this case is in violation of the French word order. In contrast, English learners of French followed their native language's word order. If the habits of the learners' first language is the driving force, why were they not bi-directional here? In other words, contrastive analysis is applicable to explain the erroneous production of English learners but not for French learners' correct use of the English order in their production.

In addition, second language learners' errors are not always caused by their first language. Second language learners make the same errors as the ones children make when they develop their first language. For example, learners of English often make an error like "He comed yesterday," imposing regularity on an irregular verb, so-called *overgeneralization*. Children whose first language is English often make the same error. In other words, this type of error is not caused by second language learners' first language. Rather, it is called *developmental errors* in that all learners, regardless of first language and second language learners, make this type of errors as they develop the knowledge of the past tense in English.

Another assumption which could be created based on the contrastive analysis hypothesis is that second language learners with different first languages would make different errors because errors are caused by first language interference. However, analyses on learner errors show that many errors, such as omissions of certain grammatical morphemes and spelling errors, are commonly committed by English learners with different first language backgrounds.

The behaviorists' perspective on language learning and the contrastive analysis hypothesis were challenged by a great deal of empirical evidence that showed language learning could not be accounted for by habit formations.

Innativists' Perspectives on Language Learning

In the early 1960s, first language acquisition research began to demonstrate that children's utterances were not just imitations and analogy. Children are observed to be born with an innate facility that guides their language learning and the ability is not affected by the kinds of conditions that are the premise of behaviorism. Chomsky (1959), one of the most influential linguists, is at the center of this position. He argued that children are born with the equipment which specifically works for language learning, and this is called *language acquisition device* (LAD). LAD is often described as an imaginary 'black box' that contains all and only the principles which are universal to all human languages. For the language acquisition device to work, children need access only to samples of the language. Principles all human languages share are called *Universal Grammar*.

• **Universal Grammar (UG)**

In this framework, language production and comprehension are based on an abstract linguistic system, a mental representation of grammar (syntax, morphology, phonology, and semantics). This kind of knowledge is unconscious and much of this knowledge does not have to be learned in the course of first language acquisition. Rather, it is derived from Universal Grammar (UG). The theory underlying UG assumes that language consists of a set of abstract *principles* that characterizes core grammars of all natural human languages. In addition to principles that are invariables, there are *parameters* that vary across languages.

Cook (1997) made an interesting explanation of these principles and parameters, using the driving of a car as an example:

> Overall there is a principle that drivers have to keep consistently to one side of the road, which is taken for granted by all drivers in all countries. Exceptions to this principle, such as people driving down motorways on the wrong side, rate stories in the media or car chases in action movies. This principle does not, however, say, which side of the road people should drive on. A parameter of driving allows the side to be the left in England and Japan, and the right in the USA and France. Once a country has opted for one side or the other, it sticks to its choice: a change of setting is a massively complex operation… for the individual travelling from England to France. So, a universal principle and a variable parameter together sum up the essence of driving. The principle states the universal requirements on driving; the parameter specifies the variation between countries.
>
> (Cook, 1997, pp. 250–251)

• UG in First Language Acquisition

What does UG have to do with child language acquisition? UG is claimed as an innate language facility which specifies the limits of a possible language. The supporting evidence of existence of UG derives from the fact that children cannot attain the complexities of adult grammars on the basis of language input alone. Children come to know certain properties of grammar that are not obviously learnable from input. In other words, there is a mismatch between the input that children are exposed to and their *ultimate attainment*, and this is called *the logical problem of language acquisition*, or the problem of *the poverty of the stimulus*. White's (1989) data provide supporting evidence. Consider the following examples:

1. I want to go.
2. I wanna go.
3. John wants to go but we don't want to.
4. John wants to go but we don't wanna.
5. Do you want to look at the chickens?
6. Do you wanna look at the chickens?
7. Who do you want to see?
8. Who do you wanna see?

Examples 1-8 show the cases where 'want to' is replaced by 'wanna.' However, there are many instances where 'want to' cannot be replaced by 'wanna,' as in examples 9-12:

9. Who do you want to feed the dog?
10. *Who do you wanna feed the dog?
11. Who do you want to win the race?

12. *Who do you wanna win the race?

White (1989) argued that even without any instruction about the grammatical rule addressed by the above examples, children are able to figure out where to use 'wanna' and where not to use 'wanna.' However, it is difficult to determine the correct use of 'want to' and 'wanna' in informal English based only on the input children are exposed to. White explained that UG guides children to understand the rules governing the distribution of these English forms. In other words, sentence 7 can be represented by something like "You want to see X" and 9 by something like "You want X to feed the dog." In 7, 'want' and 'to' are adjacent, thereby allowing contraction, but not in 9. UG leads children not to make sentences like 10 and 12.

In addition, children acquire the basic syntax and morphology of the language spoken to them in a variety of conditions. Furthermore, although language input children are exposed to is sometimes ungrammatical, they eventually acquire the correct grammar. This is seen as support for the hypothesis that human beings have an innate mechanism which is exclusively for language acquisition.

• UG in Second Language Acquisition

While Chomsky did not provide specific claims about how UG theory accounted for second language acquisition, other linguists have argued that UG provides the best framework to understand second language acquisition. UG is still accessible in second language learning and the driving force of second language learning. Cook (2003) and others assert the availability of UG by pointing out the learnability issue – *logical problem of second language acquisition*. That is, second language learners eventually know more about the language than they could reasonably have learned.

According to UG theory, when it comes to second language learning, learners need to work on parameter resetting. For example, all natural languages have the grammatical subject (i.e., principle). However, whether or not the use of the subject in declarative sentences is compulsory varies across the languages (i.e., parameter). In English, it is possible to say 'He speaks' but impossible to say 'Speaks': declarative sentences must have subjects. This is true for French, for German, and for many other languages. However, in Italian, while it is possible to say 'Il parla' (he talks), it is far more usual to say 'Parla' (talks) without an expressed subject: declarative sentences are not required to have the subject. The same is true for Chinese, Arabic, and many other languages. This variation is called 'pro-drop' parameter. In pro-drop languages like Italian and Chinese, the use of subject is not compulsory while, in non-pro-drop languages such as English and German, the subject must always be presented. The pro-drop parameter variation has effects on the grammar of all languages. That is, each of them is either pro-drop or non-pro-drop.

Learners whose first language falls into pro-drop languages need to reset the pro-drop parameter when they learn a second language which is a non-pro-drop language. In the same vein, learners whose second language is a non-pro-drop language need to reset the parameter when they learn a second language which is a pro-drop language. Then, what do learners need when they reset the parameter? Two different answers to this question have been proposed within the UG framework. The necessity of negative evidence in order to reset the parameter is at the center of this argument. Many linguists are convinced that all a child needs to learn the first language is positive evidence in the shape of an actual sentence. Like first language learning, Schwartz (1993) and other scholars claim second language learners only need positive evidence, which will eventually lead learners to adjust the parameter to second language rules. In contrast, White (1991) and other colleagues assert that negative evidence is facilitative in second language learning since it can be used to work out what does not occur in the second language. In other words, second language learners will be able to benefit from negative evidence in the process of the parameter resetting. Although these two positions have different opinions about the role of *negative evidence* in second language learning, they all agree that the UG principles are not consciously learned; the parameter settings probably need little attention. The teacher needs to focus on providing data which students can use to set the values of parameters.

• Second Language Learning Theory within UG: The Monitor Model

An early yet influential model of learning in second language literature is known as the Monitor Model, proposed by Stephen Krashen (1982). Although Krashen did not mention the connection in his writing, Monitor Model seems to be connected to Chomsky's theory of learning, adopting the

30

notion of language acquisition device (LAD). There are five hypotheses in this model: (a) acquisition-learning hypothesis, (b) monitor hypothesis, (c) natural order hypothesis, (d) input hypothesis, and (e) affective filter hypothesis.

Acquisition-learning hypothesis

Krashen (1982) claimed that second language learners have two independent means of developing knowledge of a second language: *acquisition* and *learning*.

> Acquisition [is] a process similar, if not identical to the way children develop ability in their first language. Language acquisition is a subconscious process; language acquirers are not usually aware of the fact that they are acquiring language··· The result of language acquisition, acquired competence, is also subconscious. We are generally not consciously aware of the rules of the languages we have acquired. Instead, we have a "feel" for correctness. Grammatical sentences "sound" right, or "feel" right, and errors feel wrong, even if we do not consciously know what rule was violated··· In nontechnical terms, acquisition is "picking up" a language.
>
> The second way to develop competence in a second language is by language learning. We will use the term "learning" henceforth to refer to conscious knowledge of a second language, knowing the rules, being aware of them, and being able to talk about them. In nontechnical terms, learning is "knowing about" a language, known to most people as "grammar" or "rules." Some synonyms include formal knowledge of a language or explicit learning.
>
> (Krashen, 1982, p. 10)

According to Krashen, not only does language development

take place in two distinctive ways, but learners also use the language developed through these two systems for different purposes. Learners draw on acquired unconscious knowledge in spontaneous language use. The acquisition system generates utterances and learners' attention is on meaning not form. In contrast, the learned system is used to monitor the acquired system, checking the correctness of the utterances against the knowledge in the learned system. Since these two systems are internalized differently, they can never interact. In other words, learned knowledge cannot be converted into acquired knowledge via some kind of practice. This may explain why learners may 'know' rules but may nevertheless be unable to 'use' them in spontaneous production. Conversely, learners may use a structure accurately and spontaneously but be unable to articulate the rule for its use. For this reason, Krashen argues that the effects of explicit instruction including error correction are peripheral; thus, such pedagogical approaches should be abandoned.

Monitor hypothesis

This hypothesis determines the role of the learned system. It serve as an inspector of learners' utterances generated by the acquired system. However, the monitor cannot be used at all times. There are three conditions that should be satisfied to activate the monitor, but they are necessary conditions not sufficient ones because the monitor may not be activated even when all three conditions have been met (Krashen, 1982). The three conditions are as follows:

1. Time: Learners need time to consciously think about the rules.

2. Focus on form: Learners must be paying attention to form.
3. Know the rule: Learners must have an appropriate learned system.

Therefore, according to Krashen, learners can use the learned system only when they have sufficient time to consult their rule knowledge and the task requires them to attend to accuracy. Some possible instances where these conditions are met would be the cases where learners are engaged with an untimed writing assignment or a fill-in-the-blank exercise. Since these kinds of activities are not important in overall language use, within the Monitor Model, the role of monitor is negligible.

Natural order hypothesis

This hypothesis claims that elements of language (or language rules) are acquired in a predictable order. The order cannot be changed by instruction. The natural order was determined by a synthesis of the results of the morpheme order studies. Research in both first and second language acquisition reported that learners follow sequences in their acquisition of specific linguistic features, such as the grammatical morphemes, negations, and others (Bloom, 1991; Brown, 1973; Wode, 1981). According to Krashen, these regularities take place because acquisition is guided by the innate language acquisition faculty. Thus, the order is a result of the acquired system, without interference from the learned system.

Input hypothesis

It is a supplement to the natural order hypothesis. If there is a natural order of acquisition, how is it that learners move from one point to another? The input hypothesis provides the answer. Second languages are acquired "by understanding messages, or by receiving 'comprehensible input'" (Krashen, 1985, p. 2). *Comprehensible input* contains languages slightly beyond the current level of the learner's internalized knowledge. Language containing structures a learner already knows essentially serve no purpose in acquisition. In the same vein, languages containing structures way ahead of a learner's current knowledge are not beneficial since she does not have the ability to do anything with these structures. In order to explain the notion of comprehensible input, Krashen introduces two constructs: i, which refers to a learner's current level, and 'i+1' which refers to a level just beyond the learner's current level. Thus, the input learners are exposed to must be at the 'i+1' level in order for it to be useful for language acquisition. "We move from i, our current level to i+1, the next level along the natural order, by understanding input containing i+1" (Krashen, 1985, p. 2). In Krashen's view, comprehensible input is not just a necessary condition but the sufficient condition. In other words, if there is comprehensible input, second language acquisition is an inevitable outcome.

The input hypothesis has some pedagogical implications. First, speaking is a result of acquisition. Speech cannot be taught but develops on its own as a result of building competence through comprehensible input. Thus, forcing learners to produce before they are ready can even hinder learners from processing input, taking their focus away from comprehension. Second, if input is understood, and there is enough of it, the necessary grammar is automatically provided.

The teacher does not need to attempt to teach the structure along the natural order. In other words, roughly tuned input will automatically include several levels of input including i+1 and probably i−1 and i+2, etc., as well. As long as learners are exposed to rich and comprehensible input, they will naturally access and use what they need. Therefore, the teacher's main role is to ensure that learners receive comprehensible input.

Affective filter hypothesis

The effects of learners' emotional factors on second language learning have been well documented in second language literature and most learners have experienced the role of their emotional states in second language learning. Affective filter hypothesis is one of the early theories explaining the relationship between learners' emotions and second language learning. Affect includes factors such as motivation, attitude, self-confidence, and anxiety. Indeed, the hypothesis is intended to account in large part for why some people are able to learn second languages successfully while others are not.

In Krashen's view, the lack of second language learning, as seen in the input hypothesis, is due to the dearth of comprehensible input. Comprehensible input is considered a sufficient condition where second language acquisition takes place. Then, how can it be explained that not all learners are successful despite being exposed to sufficient comprehensible input? Inappropriate affects are to blame. Learners who are motivated, have a positive attitude toward language learning, and feel comfortable and confident have their filters set low, and, if the input is comprehensible, the input will reach the language acquisition device and acquisition will take place.

In contrast, learners who are demotivated, have a negative attitude, and feel anxious and unconfident will raise their affective filters, and this will prevent input from passing through although the input is comprehensible. If the input is prevented from passing through, there can be no acquisition.

According to Krashen, the affective filter is responsible for individual differences in second language acquisition. It also differentiates child language acquisition from second language acquisition because the affective filter is not something children have.

Critics on Krashen's view

Krashen's Monitor Model has been challenged by many other scholars. One of the issues questioned is whether or not learners develop two independent systems. Krashen clearly states that what has been learned cannot become part of the acquired system. However, a significant amount of theoretical and empirical research has reported that learners are able to use the learned second language knowledge spontaneously and unconsciously through practices (DeKeyser, 1998; Segalowitz, 2003). In other words, although learners have different ways of internalizing information (i.e., *implicit* vs. *explicit learning*), the knowledge acquired through different means is not completely disconnected.

Second, Krashen's natural order hypothesis was based on studies of English morpheme acquisition. However, individual variations in the acquisition order have been observed (Goldschneider & DeKeyser, 2001), and this claim has weakened the natural order hypothesis.

The input hypothesis has also been questioned due to the

ambiguity of the concept of 'i+1.' More specifically, in order to test out the input hypothesis, it is necessary to define the exact level of 'i' and 'i+1.' However, Krashen (1982) only mentioned that "We acquire by understanding language that contains structure a bit beyond our current level of competence (i+1). This is done with the help of context or extralinguistic information" (p. 21). Also, he added that there has to be sufficient quantity of the appropriate input. But, how can we judge whether input is sufficient or not? Furthermore, how extralinguistic information could possibly aid actual acquisition of a language rule is also questionable. Krashen equates comprehension with acquisition. However, we all know that understanding a story is not equal to acquiring language forms there. We can still understand the story without knowing the language rules there. Gregg (1984) also noted that he "find[s] it difficult to imagine extra-linguistic information that would enable one to 'acquire' the third person singular -s, or yes/no questions, or indirect object placement, or passivization" (p. 88).

Although there have been many criticisms about the hypotheses that Krashen put forth, it is necessary to acknowledge the significant contributions the Monitor Model has made to the field of second language acquisition. The hypotheses have spurred a great deal of research and taken the field many steps forward. In addition, Krashen's theory made a great effect on second language teaching during a period where meaning-focused instruction replaced exclusively form-focused instruction (e.g., emphasizing learning rules or memorizing dialogues). Since then, meaning-focused instruction such as *communicative language teaching* and *content-based instruction* has been broadly employed. Krashen's hypotheses, especially the idea of comprehensible input, have been tested in second language classrooms, and some studies have found that comprehensible input without *explicit instruction* results in a great deal of progress in second language acquisition. However, studies have also proved that comprehensible input is necessary but not sufficient for second language acquisition to take place. Learning theories presented in the rest of this chapter will explain why this may be so.

Cognitivists' Views on Language Acquisition

Like the field of linguistics, the field of cognitive psychology has significantly influenced the study of second language acquisition. Cognitive psychologists claim that there is no specific module for language acquisition, and language learning occurs in the same way other learning takes places, employing the general ability for learning.

• Information Processing Models

One of the well-known cognitive psychology theories is information processing approaches which emerged in the field of psychology in the 1970s. Initially, it was a reaction to behaviorist theories that accounted for human learning only through stimulus-response behaviors. The information processing theory considers the human mind a symbolic processor that continuously works on mental processes. According to information processing approaches, attention is central to process the information, but attentional capacity is limited. Thus, when we process the incoming new information, we need to pay attention to it. If we use up all of our attentional capacity to process the new information, we cannot process other information although it is abundant around us. Gradually, through experience and practice, the information that was new becomes easier to process, and we become able to attend to other incoming information. Using more technical terms, *controlled processing* is the initial stage of processing of new information, which is a conscious and effortful process. Controlled processing becomes *automatic processing* via practice, and automatic processes require small effort and take up few cognitive resources.

In information processing approaches, second language learning also goes through the same processes. Second language learners have to pay attention at first to any aspect of the language that they are trying to understand and produce. Since there is a limit to how much information learners can attend to, learners naturally attend to the main words in a message to understand the meaning. They seldom notice grammatical morphemes attached to some of the words, especially those that do not significantly affect meaning. Through experiences and practice, learners become able to understand it quickly and even automatically, which enables them to attend to other aspects of the language. Note that the 'practice' required for the development of automaticity embraces a broad meaning. It does not mean just mechanical drills and limited production of language. Practice also includes plenty of exposure to, and comprehension of, a language feature.

Automaticity and proceduralization through practice

Skill acquisition theory, a particular kind of information processing theory, has been prolific since the mid-1980s (Bialystock & Sharwood Smith, 1985; McLaughlin, 1987). According to skill acquisition theory, learning, including language learning, starts with *declarative* or *explicit knowledge* (i.e., knowledge of that). Through practice, declarative knowledge becomes *procedural* or *implicit knowledge* (i.e., knowledge of how). It should be noted that the learning of skill is assumed to start with the explicit provision of relevant declarative knowledge. This process is called proceduralization and automatization. In second language classrooms, learners begin with explanations explicitly presented by their teachers or in textbooks and, through practice, this knowledge can convert into procedural/implicit knowledge.

Restructuring

Restructuring is the process of self-reorganization of grammar knowledge representation. This takes place when qualitative changes occur in a learner's internal representation of the second language. McLaughlin (1990) described restructuring in first language acquisition in the following way: "Restructuring is characterized by discontinuous, or qualitative change as the child moves from stage to stage in development. Each new stage constitutes a new internal organization and not merely the addition of new structural elements" (p. 117). This also explains the process of restructuring in second language acquisition. In sum, restructuring involves knowledge changes that can be large or small, abrupt or gradual, but always qualitative related to progress or development. However, the development in the notion of restructuring should not be equated with increased accuracy.

The view that development does not always mean increasing accuracy is clear in the notion of *U-shaped behavior*, which is destabilization as a consequence of restructuring. The process is defined as "the appearance of correct, or nativelike, forms at an early stage of development which then undergo a process of attrition, only to be reestablished at a later stage" (Sharwood Smith & Kellerman, 1989, p. 220). That is, U-shaped behavior reflects three stages of linguistic use. In the earliest stage, a learner produces a linguistic form correctly. At Stage 2, a learner appears to lose what she knows at Stage 1 – producing the form incorrectly. At Stage 3, like Stage 1, there is again a correct use of the form. In U-shaped learning pattern, the linguistic products of the final stage (Stage 3) cannot be differentiated from those of the first stage (Stage 1), as both are apparently targetlike. However, the underlying representation at Stage 1 and at Stage 3 are qualitatively different. In the first stage, the correct use of the form is fairly coincidental while the accurate use of the form in the final stage is based on the full representation of target-like functions and meanings.

Lightbown's (1983) study thoroughly documented U-shaped behavior as shown by French learners of English in a classroom context. She examined the use of the '-ing' form in English among sixth, seventh, and the eighth grade learners. Sixth grade learners when describing a picture said

"He is taking a cake," but at seventh grade they responded to the same picture, saying "He take a cake." They correctly used the '-ing' form at sixth grade, but they did not at seventh grade. Then, how can we account for this apparent decrease in knowledge? Lightbown explained that the present progressive was the only verb form introduced at sixth grade. With nothing else in English to compare it to, they equated it with the simple present of French. Since there was no other comparable form in their system, learners not only used the present progressive in the contexts where the '-ing' form was appropriate, but they also overused the present progressive form in the contexts in which the simple present was appropriate. When the simple present was introduced, they not only had to learn the new form, but they also had to readjust their knowledge about the present progressive. Such readjustment and restructuring resulted in a decline in both use and accuracy, called *back-sliding*. Once they had appropriate knowledge of both the present progressive and the simple present, they were able to use the present progressive only in the contexts where the form was appropriate. Lightbown (1985) provides the following rationale for restructuring:

> [Restructuring] occurs because language is a complex hierarchical system whose components interact nonlinear ways. Seen in these terms, an increase in error rate in one area may reflect an increase in complexity or accuracy in another, followed by overgeneralization of a newly acquired structure, or simply by a sort of overload of complexity which forces a restructuring, or at least a simplification, in another part of the system.
>
> (Lightbown, 1985, p. 177)

• **Learner Languages from Cognitive Views**

Cognitive approach takes a different position in explaining learner languages. As opposed to behaviorist view which sees learner language as a faulty imitation of the target language, cognitive approach views learner language as a system which has its own rules. This idea is situated in the coinage of the technical term *interlanguage* (Selinker, 1972). Interlanguage refers to the language system that each learner constructs at any given point in the development. This concept validates learners' language, "not as a deficit system, that is, a language filled with random errors, but as a system of its own with its own structure" (Gass & Selinker, 2008, p. 14). Interlanguage has some elements of the native language and the *target language*. There are also some characteristics all or most interlanguage systems share (e.g., the omission of function words). Interlanguage is systematic but also dynamic, constantly developing as learners receive more input and revise their hypotheses about the target language. However, the path through language acquisition is not necessarily smooth and even. Learners sometimes show gradual or even sudden improvement but sometimes reach a plateau for a while before something fuels further progress. Selinker (1972) also coined the term *fossilization* which generally refers to the cessation of learning.

Due to the difficulty in determining when learning has ceased, some researchers like Long (2003) note that it seems more appropriate to use the term *stabilization* of linguistic forms, rather than fossilization. In second language acquisition, it is often observed that learners reach plateaus that are far from the target language norms. Furthermore, it appears to be the case that their interlanguages become fossilized or stabilized no matter what they do in terms of further exposure to the target language. Then, the next question naturally arising is what causes fossilization. A primary causal factor is the native language influence, but this is not the only reason. Han (2004) notes that "fossilization is internally determined due to the constant functioning of maturational and native language constraints, yet it can be modulated (aggravated or alleviated) by environmental, social, and psychological forces" (p. 43).

Error analysis

Until the late 1960s, second language learners' speeches were seen as incorrect versions of the target language. In this paradigm, according to the contrastive analysis hypothesis, learners' errors were assumed to be the result of transfer of their first language. However, as mentioned previously, not all errors made by second language learners can be explained in terms of first language transfer. A great deal of research proves that many learner errors can be explained better in terms of learners' developing knowledge of the structure of the target language (i.e., *developmental errors* or *intralingual errors*) rather than the use of first language patterns (i.e., interference errors, transfer errors, or interlingual errors).

The changed view on learner languages naturally resulted in the shift in the interpretation of learner errors. Errors are not to be viewed solely as a product of flawed learning. Rather, errors are seen as windows onto a system, that is, evidence of the state of a learner's knowledge of the second language. In other words, they are viewed as "indications of a learner's attempt to figure out some system, that is, to impose regularity on the language the learner is exposed to" (Gass & Selinker, 2008, p. 102).

Along with the criticisms against the contrastive analysis hypothesis and the accompanying emphasis on the learner language system, a new approach to analyze learner errors emerged, and this is called *error analysis*. Error analysis is a type of linguistic analysis that focuses on the errors learners made. While contrastive analysis makes a comparison between the target language and the first language, in error analysis, the comparison is made between the errors a learner makes in producing the target language and the target language form itself. A number of studies were carried out in second language classrooms using error analysis, and the goal was to offer pedagogical remediation.

Error analysis largely classifies the source of errors into two types, *interlingual errors* and *intralingual errors*. While interlingual errors are those which can be attributed to the first language, intralingual errors are those which are due to the language being learned. In other words, intralingual errors do not have to do with learners' first language and it can be expected that those errors occur from speakers of a wide range of first languages. However, it is often difficult to determine the source of errors. Error analysis evidently describes what learners actually do rather than what they might do, but it does not always offer clear insights into why they do.

Another major criticism of error analysis is directed to its heavy reliance on errors. In other words, error analysis is solely based on errors learners actually made. However, it is easily observed that learners tend to avoid using certain linguistic features they perceive to be difficult for them (Schachter, 1974). This avoidance may lead to the absence of certain errors. If there is no error, it is difficult to analyze learners' interlanguage development.

In sum, cognitive approaches have made significant changes in the perspectives on learner language and put a great emphasis on the role of attention in second language learning. Under the influence of such standpoints, many second language learning theories have been proposed. The following sections will present some major theories influenced by cognitive perspectives.

Input, Interaction, Output, and Attention in Second Language Acquisition

No one would argue that language learning, regardless of first and second language, can take place without input. Input is essential for second language acquisition, but it does not mean that being exposed to input guarantees learning. In order for second language acquisition to take place, input needs to be internalized by learners. Then, what helps learners to internalize the input they receive? This section will discuss the answers based on theories related to input, interaction, and output.

• Input in Language Acquisition

As mentioned in the previous section, the earliest conceptualization of second language learning was based on a behaviorist's view in which the major driving force of language learning is the language which learners are exposed to. In this view, since imitation of the input learners are exposed to is seen as the prime mechanism, the language that surrounds learners is of critical importance. However, plenty of empirical evidence showed that language learning is not just about the language examples; it has more to do with the learner. In this sense, Corder (1967) makes a significant distinction between *input* and *intake*. Input refers to what is available to the learner, whereas intake refers to what is actually internalized or processed by the learner. Anyone who has learned second language would be familiar with the situation where the language one hears is totally incomprehensible. In this situation, there is input but not intake; it is not integrated into the current learner interlanguage system.

Researchers have been interested in the nature of the input to a language learner. Ferguson (1971) investigated language directed to linguistically deficient individuals such as young children and nonnative speakers of a language. It was found that native speakers make adjustments to their speech in the area of pronunciation, grammar, and lexicon. Ferguson named speech directed toward young children *baby talk* (known as motherese, caretaker speech, or child-directed speech) and called speech directed to nonnative speakers, *foreigner talk*. He examined the similarities between these two speech variations and found that they shared some features such as slow speech rate, loud speech, simple vocabulary, repetitions and elaboration, and dearth of slangs.

Then, what is the role played by foreigner talk in terms of language learning? It can be easily assumed that simplified input could help language learners' understanding. Without understanding the language, learning cannot take place although understanding alone cannot guarantee that language learning will occur. Parker and Chaudron (1987) reported that not all types of foreigner talk equally facilitate understanding. The discourse elaborations or modifications of the conversational interactional structures were more likely to aid comprehension than those simplifications which resulted from simplification at the linguistic level.

Input for comprehension vs. acquisition

Krashen (1983, elsewhere) claims that comprehensible input is the single most important source of second language learning. Learners gain comprehensible input mostly through listening to oral messages and reading written texts. When they process the input for meaning, grammar learning will naturally occur. However, the strong claim that comprehensible input is both necessary and sufficient for second language learning proved to be untenable in light of findings from many experimental studies (Doughty, 1991; Loschky, 1994; Sharwood Smith, 1986). The research revealed that second language learners only achieved minimal grammatical development in spite of plenty of meaningful and comprehensible input, even with young second language learners such as children attending French immersion in Canada (Swain, 1985). Input is unquestionably necessary, but it cannot be sufficient for second language acquisition.

Comprehension is crucial but it cannot guarantee language acquisition. It has been noted that comprehension and acquisition are two distinct processes. For instance, Sharwood Smith (1986) showed that simplification for the purpose of helping learners' comprehension prevents them from being exposed to a variety of language forms which could contribute to language learning. In addition, it was found that learners can comprehend more than they acquire and can acquire more than they comprehend. Such suggestive evidence of a dissociation between comprehension and acquisition calls for more empirical research which can deepen our understanding of the two.

• Interaction in Second Language Learning

The interaction approach considers that language learning takes place through input, production of language, and feedback that comes as a result of interaction (Gass & Mackey, 2006). Gass (2003) notes that interaction research "takes as its strong point the assumption that language learning is stimulated by communicative pressure, and examines the relationship between communication and acquisition and the mechanisms (e.g., noticing, attention) that mediate between them" (p. 224). Gass' brief explanation about interaction research vividly shows the components involved in interaction and they are all related to language learning.

49

Interaction hypothesis

The role of interaction in second language acquisition has been extensively discussed and investigated ever since Long (1983) proposed the Interaction Hypothesis. The hypothesis was based on the research which investigated the interaction between college-level English second language learners and English native-speaking pre-service and in-service teachers. He extended Krashen's proposal of comprehensible input by analyzing actual discourse occurring between non-native speakers (NNSs) and native-speakers (NSs). Long agreed with Krashen in that comprehensible input is important. However, he departed from Krashen's approach by focusing on what made input comprehensible. He proposed that the best kind of comprehensible input learners can obtain is input that has been modified through interaction. In other words, interactional modifications resulting from the adjustments after receiving some signals that the interlocutor needs help to clearly understand the message make input comprehensible; thus, interaction facilitates second language learning.

Interactional modification is initiated by comprehension problems. When people communicate, if they do not clearly understand each other, they strive to make meaning more comprehensible for each other. In other words, they are *negotiating for meaning*. Negotiation refers to communication in which the participants' attention is focused on resolving a communication problem. Negotiation episodes typically begin with clarification requests if non-understanding is serious (e.g., What do you mean? Pardon me?), confirmation checks if a listener is somewhat unsure if she has understood the message correctly (e.g., You mean X?), and comprehension checks if a speaker is not sure whether the other interlocutor has not understood what she has said (e.g., You know what I mean? Do you want me to repeat?). The following examples show how input becomes comprehensible through negotiation:

Example 1.3

(picture description)

Jane:	All right now [reading from the script], above the sun place the squirrel. He's right on the top of the sun.
Hiroshi:	What is … the word?
Jane:	OK. The sun.
Hiroshi:	Yeah, sun, but
Jane:	Do you know what the sun is?
Hiroshi:	Yeah, of course. Wh–what's the
Jane:	Squirrel. Do you know what a squirrel is?
Hiroshi:	No.
Jane:	OK. You've seen them running around on campus. They're little furry animals. They're short and brown and they eat nuts like crazy.

(Gass & Varonis, 1994, p. 296)

The following episode between a native speaker (NS) and a nonnative speaker (NNS) shows how negotiation takes place and the excerpt from the interview with the NNS shows how this negotiation helps his understanding (Mackey, 2012):

Example 1.4

NNS: Does he has some hair?

NS: He has a little bit of hair.

NNS: A little bit? What do you mean a little bit?

NS: He has twelve of them.

NNS: He is twelve? What does it mean?
NS: He has twelve hairs on his head.
NNS: What does it mean he has twelve hair?
NS: On his head he has one, two, three, four··· twelve hairs
NNS: OK

Excerpt from stimulated recall interview with the NNS in Example 1.4

So I asked her and she says a number and I still not understood so again I have ask her and this time she tell me by counting, she say one, two, three, four and so I see she is counting hair and little bit have mean small amount. It is good because when I ask her for her meaning, she can explain me, and then I can understand. First I think little bit maybe refer sides of head, now I see mean little, few, only twelve, is not many. I think have we have thousand and thousand of hair on head but in this case have only little bit. Twelve. Few.

(Mackey, 2012, p. 132)

As seen in Example 1.4 and the excerpt of the interview, the NNS did not understand the meaning of 'a little bit' at the beginning, but, through the negotiation of meaning, the NNS came to understand the meaning of it.

Long (1983, 1996) claims that interactionally modified input would be more beneficial for second language acquisition than other kinds of input such as unmodified or authentic input and pre-modified input (as in graded readers) which often means simplified input. Ortega (2009) also emphasizes the advantages of interactionally modified input:

Interactional modifications have the potential to bring about comprehension in a more individualized or learner-contingent

> fashion, with repetitions and redundancies rather than simplification. Thus, an important general benefit of interactional modifications is their contingency, in that learners are potentially engaging in what educational researchers call just-in-time learning, or learning at the right point of need.
>
> (Ortega, 2009, pp. 61-62)

Long's revised interaction hypothesis (Long, 1996) puts more emphasis on individual cognitive processing than the original version of the interaction hypothesis which focused on negotiation for meaning. In particular, noticing specific language features in the input and the role of corrective feedback are underscored.

Corrective feedback in interaction

Corrective feedback, also called *negative feedback*, may come about as a part of negotiating meaning or form, and it provides learners with crucial information about lack of success of their utterances. Long (1996) clearly points out the role of corrective feedback during negotiation for meaning:

> Environmental contributions to acquisition are mediated by selective attention and the learner's developing L2 processing capacity, and these resources are brought together most usefully although not exclusively, during *negotiation for meaning. Negative feedback* obtained during negotiation work or elsewhere may be facilitative of L2 development, at least for vocabulary, morphology, and language-specific syntax, and essentially for learning certain specifiable L1-L2 contrasts.
>
> (Long, 1996, p. 417)

53

In this view, through negotiation for meaning a learner's attention is drawn to problematic areas of knowledge or production. First, the learner may notice that what she says differs from what a native speaker (interlocutor) says, which is referred to as *noticing the gap* (Schmidt & Frota, 1986). In addition, the learner may notice that she cannot express what she wants to express, noticing a hole in her interlanguage (Swain, 1996).

Corrective feedback may help learners pay attention to the problematic areas of their language and may give them additional information relevant to the problems. Needless to say, corrective feedback can be provided in written form. However, this chapter will only deal with oral corrective feedback which takes place during interaction.

Oral corrective feedback can be classified differently depending on various categorizations. First, corrective feedback can fall into input-providing feedback or output-prompting feedback. The former provides learners with the correct form, and *recasts* and direct correction belong to this type of correction. The latter elicits a correct form from the learner, and clarification requests and elicitations are examples of this type of corrective feedback. Corrective feedback can also be classified into either implicit or explicit feedback. Implicit corrective feedback does not directly indicate that a learner makes an error (e.g., recasts and clarification reguests) while explicit feedback clearly points out that an error is committed (e.g., direct correction and metalinguistic feedback). Definitions and examples of corrective feedback are as follows (Lyster & Ranta, 1998):

1. Explicit Correction

A direct signal that an error has been committed and a correct form are provided. As the teacher provides the correct form, it is clearly indicated that what the learner said is incorrect (e.g., You should say…). An example is below:

Example 1.5

Student:	I stayed at the hotel...hmmm around hotel, there are many store.
Teacher:	Not 'are;' 'were'.
Student:	Yes, there were many shop.

(Kim, 2011, p. 83)

2. Metalinguistic Feedback

It contains comments, information, or questions related to the correctness of the learner's utterance, without explicitly offering the correct form. It can be provided in different ways. Metalinguistic feedback generally indicates that there is an error (e.g., Can you see your error?) or provides grammatical terminology related to the nature of error (e.g., Past tense is needed here) as in the example below:

Example 1.6

Student:	Later, foolish bat went into the home of another weasel.
Teacher:	Bat? Can you think about your grammar? You're talking about the same bat you talked before.

(Kim, 2016, p. 61)

3. Recasts

Recasts can be defined in many different ways, but all include two elements: maintaining the learner's intended meaning and correcting errors. Second language researchers typically define recasts as "utterances that repeat a learner's incorrect utterance, making only the changes necessary to produce a correct utterance, without changing the meaning" (Nicholas, Lightbown, & Spada, 2001, p. 732) as in the following example:

Example 1.7

NNS: The boy have many flowers in the basket.
NS: Yes, the boy has many flowers in the basket.

(Nicholas, Lightbown, & Spada, 2001, p. 721)

4. Clarification Requests

They indicate to learners that their utterance has not been understood well or the utterance is incorrect in some way (e.g., What did you say? Pardon me?). In the following example, the teacher gestures to the student to signal that the utterance is not understood or is ill-formed:

Example 1.8

Student: Eye ache
Teacher: Uh? What did you say?
Student: I have eye pain. So I see my doctor.

(Kim, 2011, p. 83)

5. Elicitation

It is used to directly elicit the correct form from the learner. The teacher elicits completion of their own utterances (e.g., You went···) or uses questions to elicit correct forms (e.g., How do you say X in English?). An example is below:

Example 1.9

Student: Actually, I saw this. When I was... New York, I visited MoMa art gallery. I see, I saw this. It is more than beautiful than this one.

Techer:	More...
Student:	Ah, more than, more beautiful than this.

(Kim, 2011, p. 84)

6. Repetition

The teacher repeats the learner's erroneous utterances. In most cases, the teacher puts some prosodic stress on the incorrect form to raise the learner's awareness of the incorrectness. See the example below:

Example 1.10

Student:	I went to Kim-bab Chunkguk. Yesterday, my sister call from Korea University, so I go there.
Teacher:	You **go** there?
Student:	Yes. She and I together.

(Kim, 2011, p. 83)

7. Combined Feedback

The teacher sometimes uses various strategies simultaneously to correct learners' errors as seen in the example below:

Example 1.11

Student:	Yes, I don't do the shopping a lot of time.
Teacher:	A lot of time? All the time. (repetition + recast)
Student:	Yes, only Sunday.

(Kim, 2011, p. 83)

The role of oral corrective feedback has been extensively investigated in the field of second language acquisition. Not all studies found corrective feedback to be effective in second language learning, but several meta-analyses (Li, 2010; Lyster & Saito, 2010; Mackey & Goo, 2007) have proved that it has a facilitative role. However, teachers are still facing longstanding issues in practicing corrective feedback in the second language classroom. Chaudron (1988) identified five questions that need to be considered: (a) Should learner errors be corrected? (b) When should learner errors be corrected? (c) Which learner errors should be corrected? (d) How should learner errors be corrected? (e) Who should correct learner errors? These pedagogical questions will be discussed in Chapter 5.

• Output in Second Language Learning

Interaction involves not only input but also production, output. By the mid-1980s, it was becoming ostensible that plenty of input was crucial but not sufficient for second language acquisition to take place. It was at this juncture that Swain (1983) formulated comprehensible output hypothesis, also called pushed output hypothesis and output hypothesis. This hypothesis was based on her research into language development of students attending French immersion schools (Swain, 1983, 1985). The studies revealed that learners had optimal comprehension abilities and content learning as well as discourse competence; however, they lacked grammatical competence in spite of their prolong exposure to comprehensible input in meaning-oriented classrooms. Swain concluded what had been missing in immersion schools were sufficient opportunities for the students to use the language in a meaningful way.

One of the reasons why input alone is not sufficient for language acquisition is because when one hears language, one can often interpret the meaning without the use of syntax. For instance, if one hears only the words 'man, set, and fire,' she can easily assume that 'a man set the fire' without thinking of the word order. In addition, when one hears the sentence 'I worked yesterday,' she may hear 'yesterday' and understand the interlocutor is talking about the event that happened in the past without processing the grammatical morpheme '-ed.' In other words, comprehension does not usually demand the full processing of forms. It is possible to understand the meaning of a message by counting on content words with aid of contextual clues, world knowledge, and guessing.

However, this is not the case with language production. When we produce language, we need to put the words into some order. Put differently, production "may force the learner to move from semantic processing to syntactic processing" (Swain, 1985, p. 249). Particularly, if the interlocutors do not understand, learners may push themselves to deliver their intended meaning more precisely, and this is called comprehensible output. Comprehensible output refers to the need for a learner to be "pushed toward the delivery of a message that is not only conveyed, but that is conveyed precisely, coherently, and appropriately" (Swain, 1985, p. 249). See the following episode and recall comments:

Example 1.12: Pushed Output

NNS: And in hand in hand have a bigger glass to see.
NS: It's err. You mean, something in his hand?
NNS: Like spectacle. For older person.
NS: Mmmm, sorry I don't follow, it's what?
NNS: In hand have he have has a glass for looking through for make the print bigger to see, to see the print, for magnify.
NS: He has some glasses?
NNS: Magnify glasses he has magnifying glass.

NS: Oh aha I see a magnifying glass, right that's a good one, OK.

Excerpt from stimulated recall interview with the NNS in Example 1.12

In this example I see I have to manage my errerr expression because he does not understand me and I cannot think of exact word right then. I am thinking thinking it is nearly in my mind, thinking bigger and magnificate and eventually magnify. I know I see this word before but so I am sort of talking around around this word but he is forcing me to think harder, think harder for the correct word to give him so he can understand and so I was trying. I carry on talking until finally I get it, and when I say it, then he understand it, me.

(Mackey, 2012, pp. 132–133)

Example 1.12 and the interview show that the NNS realized that his initial utterance was not understood. Pushed to reformulate his initial utterance, the NNS modifies his output to facilitate the NS's understanding.

In addition to the function of output of pushing learners to produce more accurate sentence, Swain (1985) proposes three other functions of output in second language learning: hypothesis testing, automaticity, and feedback.

The following example shows how learners test their own hypotheses through output:

Example 1.13

NNS: poi unbicchiere (then a glass)

INT: unche, come? (a what, what?)

NNS: bicchiere (glass)

Excerpt from stimulated recall interview with the NNS in Example 1.13

I was drawing a blank. Then I thought of a vase but then I thought that since there was no flower, maybe it was just a big glass. So, then I thought I'll say and see.

(Mackey, Gass, & McDonough, 2000)

In this episode, the nonnative speaker was involved in interactions which were videotaped. Right after, he was interviewed using video as a prompt. The retrospective comments, in particular, "I'll say and see" demonstrated that the learner was testing the accuracy of his knowledge.

Another piece of evidence that shows that learners test hypotheses through production is self-correction. In the following episode, it appears that both Hiroko and Izumi are trying to find out the right form:

Example 1.14

Hiroko:	A man is uh drinking c–coffee or tea un with un the scucer of the uh uh coffee set is uh in his un knee.
Izumi:	In him knee.
Hiroko:	Uh on his knee.
Izumi:	Yeah.

(Gass & Varonis, 1989, p. 81)

Output also promotes automaticity. Automatic processing results from "consistent mapping of the same input to the same pattern of activation over many trials" (McLaughlin, 1987, p. 134). In other words, practice is essential to achieve automaticity, production is a good way of practice; thus, output plays an integral role in automaticity. Output, needless to say, provides learners with opportunities to receive corrective feedback.

• Attention in Second Language Learning

Attention has been seen as one of the key mechanisms that mediates between input and learning. Second language learners are exposed to more input than they can process; thus, they need some help to sort through the massive amount of input. Gass, Svetics, and Lemelin (2003) accounts for "language processing is like other kinds of processing: Humans are constantly exposed to and often overwhelmed by various sorts of external stimuli and are able to, through attentional devices, 'tune in' some stimuli and 'tune out' others" (p. 498). In other words, attention is conceived as the mechanism that allows learners to process a portion of the input they receive.

In order to understand how attention affects second language learning processes, we need to have a general understanding of the main characteristics of attention. One main characteristic of attention is that its capacity is limited. We are not able to attend to all information. Since attention is limited, it is thought to be selective. In addition, attention can be voluntary in the sense that it can be subject to cognitive control that is driven by goals and intentions of the individual.

In the field of second language acquisition, how attention affects second language learning has been investigated by examining the quality of attention that is necessary for second language learning. The focus has been drawn to the learning process and outcome under three conditions: incidental learning, implicit learning, and explicit learning. *Incidental learning* refers to learning without intention, while doing something else. The learning of second language vocabulary during pleasure reading is an incidental type of learning that has been found to be possible. This is also what Krashen (2004) regards as crucial for language acquisition, and some of the recent work such as Horst (2005) proves the role of incidental learning in second language acquisition. Of course, we cannot rule out learning without intention, but people learn faster, more and better when they deliberately apply themselves to learning (Hulstijn & Laufer, 2001). Thus, learning with intention remains importantly in second language acquisition because of its facilitative role. *Implicit learning* includes learning with no intervention of controlled attention and without providing rules and without asking to search for rules, while *explicit learning* refers to learning with the intervention of controlled attention and, usually with provision of rules. Both learning processes are crucial and it seems unnecessary to judge which seems better than the other.

Noticing hypothesis

One of the second language theories which specifically emphasize the role of attention in learning process is Schmidt's (1990, elsewhere) Noticing Hypothesis. Schmidt (1990) argues that only attended input can be used for second language learning by saying "learning requires awareness *at the time of learning*" (Schmidt, 1995, p. 26, italics in the original). Put differently, learning cannot occur without awareness because the learner must be aware of language input in order for it to become internalized. Awareness and learning cannot be dissociated. Schmidt's Noticing Hypothesis comes from his diary studies from when he was in Brazil learning Portuguese. While he stayed in Brazil, he studied Portuguese formally (5 weeks), and spent time interacting with native speakers of Portuguese. He also kept diary records and tape-recorded himself. In order to verify the relationship between noticing and his output, his class notes and diary notes were compared with the tape recording of his speech. The data were analyzed in a number of ways. What appeared to be significant was the relationship between what he noted and the emergence of these forms in his speech. In addition, Schmidt argues that learning can be facilitative when learners notice something they hear or see in the second language that is different from what they expected, so called *noticing the gap*. Following Schmidt, a great deal of research shows the importance of awareness and attention in second language learning (Leow, 1997; Mackey, Gass, & McDonough, 2000). It can be said that attention is the mechanism that is at the heart of the Interaction Hypothesis. Negotiation and other types of corrective interaction draw learners' attention to the part of their language that is deviant from the target language form.

The theories mentioned in this section are not independent from each other, but they are rather interrelated. Input which second language learners are exposed to provides essential information. It shows what is possible (i.e., positive evidence) and what is not possible (i.e., negative evidence) in the second language. In order for such offered information to be used for learning, learners should internalize it, and this process can be facilitated by offering proper learning conditions (e.g., noticing the gap via corrective feedback through negotiation for meaning).

Sociocultural Theory

Second language learning theories based on cognitive approaches see second language interaction as a source of input to be parsed by internal learning mechanisms. In this section, we will consider a theory which takes a different view on interaction. It argues that interaction constitutes the learning process, which is essentially social rather than individual in nature, and this is called sociocultural theory. This theory takes its starting point from the work of Lev Vygotsky, a leading figure in early Soviet psychology. Vygotsky was mainly concerned with the child's development in relationship to the first language. His view on child's language growth has been developed to explain second language acquisition by second language researchers. In order to apprehend Vygotsky's perspective on language development, Lantolf (2000) suggests that one needs to understand the concept of mediation:

> The central and distinguishing concept of sociocultural theory is that higher forms of human mental activity are *mediated*. Vygotsky (1987) argued that just as humans do not act directly on the physical world but rely, instead, on tools and labour activity, we also use symbolic tools, or signs, to mediate and regulate our relationships with others and with ourselves... Included among

> symbolic tools are numbers and arithmetic systems, music, art, and above all, language. As with physical tools, humans use symbolic artifacts to establish an indirect, or mediated, relationship between ourselves and the world.
>
> (Lantolf, 2000, p. 80)

In sociocultural perspectives, learning results from mediated tools and language is the central tool for learning ('tool for thought'). Learning is also viewed as socially mediated through face-to-face interaction. Learning takes place while people jointly solve problems with experts and also with peers.

• Zone of Proximal Development

Vygotsky perceived a potential gap between the child's actual developmental stage and the stage they can reach with some help from other people. He called this the *Zone of Proximal Development* (ZPD) and defined it as "the distance between the child's actual developmental level as determined by independent problem solving and the higher level of potential development as determined through problem solving under adult guidance or in collaboration with more capable peers" (Vygotsky, 1978, p. 85). He also noted that "the only good kind of instruction is that which marches ahead of development and leads it" (Vygotsky, 1986, p. 188).

The ZPD has been developed in the field of second language acquisition. In particular, the concept of assistance is interpreted as *scaffolding*. In a second language context, scaffolding has been used in many different senses. In some cases, scaffolding includes the use of anything the learner consults such as the use of grammar books or dictionaries and teacher corrective feedback. Others maintain the original idea of Vygotsky's ZPD: scaffolding is social mediation involving two people, and is performed by a person who is an expert. In either way, according to social cultural theory, second language learners advance to higher level of linguistic knowledge when they collaborate and interact with speakers of the second language who are more knowledgeable than they are.

• Other Regulation and Self-Regulation

In sociocultural theory, successful learning involves a change from collaborative inter-mental activity to autonomous intra-mental activity. The former is called a process of *other-regulation*; that is, unskillful individuals carry out the given task with some guidelines from other more skilled individuals. Once they internalize new skills or knowledge, they become *self-regulated* people who are capable of autonomous functioning and self-management. This shift occurs through *scaffolding*, and even more effectively and successfully within the ZPD. One phenomenon which can be observed in self-regulated individuals is the use of *private speech*, talking to and for themselves. This is seen as evidence of one's ability to regulate her own behavior. Private speech, also called inner speech, reflects an advance on the earliest uses of languages, which are social and interpersonal. The completely autonomous learner has developed inner speech as a tool of thought. Learners are seen as active constructors of their own learning environment.

As noted above, initially, sociocultural theory assumes that development occurs through interaction with an interlocutor who is more knowledgeable than learners. However, some have extended scaffolding to include assistance from people at the same level (Ohta, 2001; Swain & Lapkin, 1998, 2002), and they have proved that learners are able to collaboratively construct second language knowledge in the absence of an expert knower. The following examples from García Mayo (2002) show well how two learners collaboratively interact with each other to find a correct form. The utterances they use below are called *language related episode* or *meta-talk*:

Example 1.15

Student 1:	After running up the stairs I was quite··· breath··· out of breath?...
Student 2:	Out of breath?
Student 1:	I think it is out of breath because without breath sound weird, and···
Student 2:	Yeah, out of breath sounds better

Example 1.16

Student 1:	··· mean are less incline··· it has to be an adjective··· inclined to confess, you are inclined to do something
Student 2:	To confession
Student 1:	To confess···To confess what?
Student 2:	But after a preposition··· to is a preposition
Student 1:	Yeah
Student 2:	So it should be followed by ing···
Student 1:	Inclined to confessing···
Student 2:	Yeah···

Student 1 :	No, because to is part of the second verb··· inclined to confess··· yeah
Student 2 :	Ok, I trust you

(García Mayo, 2002, p. 329)

In Examples 1.15 and 1.16, while two students are interacting, they talk about the language form ('out of breath' and 'to confess'). This kind of interaction differs from solely meaning-based interaction.

Chapter Concluding Remarks

This chapter explains the array of second language acquisition theories and how they account for learners' ability to acquire a non-primary language from different perspectives. Since they have different theoretical foundations (e.g., animal behaviors, linguistics, psychology, and sociology), they have disagreements about the key mechanism that brings about second language acquisition. Those who want to have insights into language teaching practice based on the theories of second language acquisition are often frustrated by the lack of agreement among the so-called experts. However, it also implies that the process of second language acquisition is so complicated that no single theory is sophisticated enough to provide a complete explanation about the process. In this sense, language teachers need to be eclectic, which means

69

that they consider more than one second language theory to understand the dynamic nature of second language learners and classrooms.

70

Chapter

2

Learner Individual Differences

Chapter 2.

Learner Individual Differences

One of the most widely recognized facts about second language learning is that learners greatly differ in rates and outcomes of second language learning. Many researchers have examined how individual characteristics are associated with success or lack thereof. The relationships between learning outcomes and individual differences are investigated by measuring learners' characteristics and their second language proficiency. Learner characteristics are generally measured using questionnaires and proficiency is measured by a language test. This chapter focuses on some of the important factors affecting individual differences in second language learning, which are motivation, aptitude, personality, learning styles, learning strategies, willingness to communicate, and the age at which learning begins.

Motivation

Motivation is generally understood to refer to the desire fueling second language learning and maintaining learning. It makes sense that individuals who are motivated will learn the target language faster and to a greater degree than those who are not. Furthermore, numerous studies have proved that motivation is a strong predictor of language-learning success (Dörnyei, 2001a, 2001b).

Robert Gardner is one of the important figures in the field of motivation in second language learning. Gardner (1985) argues that four elements must be present for a student to be considered motivated: a goal, desire to achieve the goal, positive attitudes, and effort. Central to this approach is the concept of integration, which refers to an individual's disposition toward the target language group and the extent to which he or she desires interaction with this group or even to become similar to that group. Masgoret and Gardner (2003) notes that integrativeness "supports an individual's motivation to learn a second language, but that motivation is responsible for achievement in the second language" (p. 124) (called *integrative motivation*). In addition, instrumental orientation (called *instrumental motivation*), generally referring to learners' pragmatic reasons for studying the language such as obtaining a job and passing a class, also contributes to language achievement. However, he puts more emphasis on integrative motivation than instrumental motivation. Gardner's socio-educational model has considerably influenced research on the relationship between motivation and second language learning. However, its generalizability has been questioned since the model was primarily developed in bilingual contexts in Canada, where integration into the second language culture is essential. In addition, in the case of English, it becomes a lingua franca, which makes the integrative aspect absent to some degree (Loewen, 2015).

Another criticism surrounding the socio-educational model is that it sees motivation as a fairly stable and consistent characteristic. However, since the 1990s, motivation research has entered a process-oriented approach. In this approach, motivation is viewed as dynamic and changing. Based on this perspective, Dörnyei and his colleagues (e.g., Dörnyei, 2005; Dörnyei & Ottó, 1998) proposed a model of motivation that allows for changes over time. In particular, the model shows how an individual learner's motivation gradually changes over time. Three terms refer to three temporal stages: preactional stage, actional stage, and postactional stage. In the preactional stage, also described as choice motivation, motivation is generated and the goal that will be pursued is selected. Actional stage, also referred to as executive motivation, relates to the sustaining of the activity. Finally, postactional stage, called motivation retrospection, follows the completion of the action and involves looking back on the activity, assessing it, and moving forward (Dörnyei, 2005). Based on this process model, Dörnyei (2001a) proposed a framework for motivational teaching practice:

▷ Creating the basic motivational condition, which involves establishing good social relations and a positive learning atmosphere

- ▷ Generating initial motivation, which involves building students' interest in and positive attitudes to learning the language
- ▷ Maintaining and protecting motivation, comprising pedagogical strategies for keeping students well motivated and involved during the learning process
- ▷ Encouraging positive retrospective self–evaluation, which entails enhancing students' self–perceptions of competence and success

Furthermore, expanding and synthesizing previous motivation research, Dörnyei (2005) formulates the second language (L2) Motivational Self System, which consists of the ideal L2 self, the ought-to L2 self, and L2 learning experience. The concept of the ideal L2 self proposes that motivation for L2 learning is enhanced if a learner sees his or her ideal self as a person who speaks a second language. In contrast, the ought-to L2 self has to do with the feelings of obligation that learners might have about L2 learning (e.g., learning a second language is something they should do). Thus, this motivation dimension may bear little resemblance to learners' own desires and wishes. Second language learning experiences refers to executive motivation related to the immediate learning environment and experience. Dörnyei (2005) further redefines integrativeness not as a drive to identify with members of the target language but as a drive to close the discrepancy between the actual self and the ideal L2 self.

Although the concepts of motivation have changed over time, there has been a continuing interest in how to motivate learners in second language classrooms. To that end, researchers have examined the motivational strategies, and

Dörnyei and Csizér (1998) suggests the following 10 principles for motivating second language students:

1. Set a personal example with your own behavior.
2. Create a pleasant, relaxed atmosphere in the classroom.
3. Present the tasks properly.
4. Develop a good relationship with the learners.
5. Increase the learners' linguistic self–confidence.
6. Make the language classes interesting.
7. Promote learner autonomy.
8. Personalize the learning process.
9. Increase the learners' goal–orientedness.
10. Familiarize learners with the target language culture.

(Adapted from Dörnyei & Csizér, 1998, p. 215)

Motivation, needless to say, is one of the driving forces that help learners to start and maintain second language learning. As noted previously, motivation has the dynamic nature. In other words, we can easily see second language learners who are highly motivated at the beginning of the learning stage being demotivated as learning advances; helping learners maintain motivation seems more challenging than triggering initial motivation.

Language Learning Aptitude

In general, aptitude refers to one's potential for learning new knowledge or skills. Aptitude specific to language learning concerns one's strengths in the cognitive processes that are involved in second language learning (Robinson, 2005). Language aptitude is also viewed as a primarily innate, fairly stable trait that is not affected by training (Li, 2013). Moreover, language aptitude has been considered one of the best predictors of language learning success (Skehan, 1989).

What constitutes language aptitude? It has been identified as having several different components. Tests developed to measure language aptitude include different elements. Nevertheless, there are some core components that are similar across views, which are called "standard 'four component' view of language aptitude" (Skehan, 1989, p. 26): phonemic coding ability, grammatical sensitivity, inductive learning ability, and memorization ability.

Phonemic coding ability refers to an ability to discriminate sounds in the input and to encode them in a manner such that they can be recalled later. Grammatical sensitivity addresses the ability that learners have to recognize the grammatical functions of words in sentences. It does not include learners' knowledge of metalinguistic terminology, but rather the ability to determine whether or not words in different sentences perform the same function. For instance, the learner is asked to find out which one, among (a) – (e) in the sentence 2, has the same function as 'him' in sentence 1:

1. I gave **him** the book.
2. When **Peter's mother** died, **Mary** wrote **a letter to him**.
   (a) (b) (c) (d) (e)

Inductive learning ability is the ability to infer or induce the rules or generalizations about language from samples of the language. In other words, it has to do with the ability to recognize the grammatical patterns and relationships that are present in the input without being taught specific, explicit grammatical rules. Lastly, memorization ability, also called *rote learning* ability, concerns the ability to make and retain sound-meaning associations. It is related to the learner ability to memorize and remember second language words and other information.

Skehan (1989) asserts that successful language learners may not be strong in all of the aspects of aptitude. For instance, individual learners may have strong abilities in language analysis but only average memories. Then, the following logical question would be whether there can be any practical applications in terms of tailoring language classrooms to the aptitude characteristics of students. Not many studies have been conducted to investigate this issue, probably due to the fact that it is difficult to isolate one factor in a complex learning environment as contributing to success or lack of success. Nevertheless, there have been a few relevant studies. For example, Wesche (1981) and Skehan (1996) reported a high level of student satisfaction when instruction was matched to learner characteristics: analytic learners did better with more analytic methodologies and memory-oriented learners did better with methodologies that included exposure to longer chunks of language.

Providing individualized instruction compatible with learner aptitude profiles would be the most beneficial for learners. However, as we all know, this is hardly applicable to second language classrooms composed of learners with different aptitude profiles, but teachers, at least, may be able to ensure that they offer a wide range of activities to accommodate learners with different aptitude profiles.

Learning Styles

Learning styles refer to "cognitive, affective, and physiological traits that are relatively stable indicators of how learners perceive, interact with, and respond to the learning environment" (Keefe, 1979, p. 4). In other words, the way we absorb and process new information and skills seem to hinge on a link between our cognition and personality.

When it comes to cognition, cognitive styles refer to "consistent individual differences in preferred ways of organizing and processing information and experience" (Messick, 1984, p. 5). Cognitive styles ultimately determine how learners approach learning tasks in second language classrooms, and they are not consciously controlled by learners. Cognitive styles are often depicted on a value-free bipolar dimension using continua, and the polarities of continua are neither good nor bad. The extreme of a cognitive style is just different rather than better or worse.

One of the cognitive styles that has been considerably studied both inside and outside second language acquisition is field dependence (FD) and field independence (FI). FD and FI cognitive styles refer to the extent to which an individual benefits from "an analytic as opposed to a global way of experiencing environment" (Keefe, 1979, p. 9). Research into FD/FI has found the relationships between FD/FI cognitive styles and various individual characteristics (Chapelle & Roberts, 1986). FD learners experience their environments globally, readily perceiving the whole picture rather than individual parts. They tend to be extrovert, externally motivated, and influenced by peer groups and authority figures. By virtue of their empathy and social outreach, they are inclined to work well in groups and seek out more opportunities to interact with other people. Due to these characteristics, they are more likely to be successful in learning the communicative aspects of language.

In contrast, FI learners look at their world analytically and easily differentiate pieces of information from the whole context within which they are embedded. FI learners tend to be intrinsic and intrinsically motivated with self-directed goals, and they prefer to structure their own learning and find solutions to problems for themselves. They typically possess less effective social skills, so they prefer to work individually (Hoffman, 1986, 1997). Thus, they are more likely to be good at learning that involves analysis, attention to details, and mastering of exercises.

In addition, some learners prefer to start with examples, so generalization can be made from the patterns (e.g., "I learn better by figuring out the rules from examples in the language") while some prefer to start with the rules or theories, so they can be applied to example (e.g., "I learn better when I have the language rules before applying them"). The former learning style is called inductive learning, and the latter is referred to as deductive learning.

Individual learners also have different perceptual orientation. Some learners prefer reading and studying charts and graphic information, and they are called visual learners. Visual learners might rewrite lecture notes using color coding or other visual organization schema. Some learners prefer to take in information auditorily, and they are referred to as auditory learners. They prefer listening to reading, so lectures are an effective means of absorbing information. And some learners, called kinesthetic learners, tend to prefer demonstrating and physical activity involving body movement. Successful learners may use both visual and auditory input, and even physical activity, but they slightly prefer one way to the other, which may distinguish one learner from another. Interestingly, Reid (1987) found that there were significant differences among learners with different first language background. For instance, Korean students were more visually oriented than native English speakers and Japanese students were the least auditorily oriented.

Research findings that individual learners have different learning styles suggest that teachers might be better able to devise style-based teaching approaches to accommodate their learners' learning styles (Dörnyei, 2005; Oxford, 1999). However, offering customized instruction is challenging for practical reasons in classrooms. As an alternative way, teachers can vary their teaching styles. For instance, teachers might employ different types of input so that one task requires students to read, another requires students to listen, and yet another requires them to work first independently and then in pairs. Another approach to learning styles might help learners gain experience operating outside their preferred styles, and this is called style stretching (Ehrman, 1996). This can be done by first examining learning styles using a questionnaire designed to raise learners' awareness of their preferred ways of learning. Then, they could engage in tasks designed to make them use a style they do not prefer. By developing the ability to respond amenably in different situations, learners are more likely to achieve success in second language learning.

Personality

Personality research, which is related to learning styles, has a long tradition in psychology. Although it is hard to categorize one's personality, extroversion/introversion is one of the characteristics commonly used in determining individuals' personality. The stereotype of introverted people is that they are much happier with a book than with other people while the extroverted people are happier with other people than with a book. These stereotypes have implications for second language learning success. Some people might think that introverted people do better in school than extroverted people, and empirical research has provided evidence for this. However, the sociability associated with extroverts easily make us assume that they would engage in more talking, and this social interaction in a second language classroom would help them develop the language. Thus, there are good reasons to think that both extroversion and introversion lead to second language learning success in different ways. The extrovert would take advantages of certain tasks and methods of language teaching while the introvert would get benefits from others.

Another commonly mentioned feature of personality is learner anxiety. Horwitz, Horwitz, and Cope (1986) defines anxiety as "the subjective feeling of tension, apprehension, nervousness, and worry associated with an arousal of the automatic nervous system" (p. 125). Many second language learners experience feelings of worry, nervousness, and stress. In early studies in learner anxiety, researchers thought anxiety as a permanent feature of one's personality. However, more recent research considers that anxiety can be temporary and context-specific. In other words, learners' feelings of nervousness depend on particular situations in which learners are. For instance, learners feel more anxious when they make oral presentations in front of the whole class than when they interact in groups. Anxiety could interfere learning process. However, some degree of tension can help learners invest extra effort and push themselves to perform better, and this is called facilitating anxiety.

Other personality characteristics such as risk-taking, self-esteem, talkativeness, and empathy have also been studied. However, the previous research has reported inconclusive results. This may be attributed to methodological problems inherent in research into personality factors. It is difficult to measure personality characteristics. Most studies have measured individuals' personality variables heavily based on their scores on personality questionnaires and related these to language proficiency tests. For instance, the questionnaires related to extroversion and introversion include such questions as "Whenever I go somewhere, I develop personal contacts" and "In a large group, I tend to keep silent" (Oxford, 1993). To some extent, these questions may measure whether an individual is extroverted or introverted. However, the answer could vary depending on the situation he or she is in. For instance, in the first question, the meaning of 'whenever I go somewhere' is ambiguous, and, in the latter question, we tend to talk more about familiar topics than unfamiliar things. In addition, the relationship between personality variables and second language learning success could be affected by the types of language proficiency tests. In other words, the relationship will vary depending on whether a study employs a test for communicative ability or grammatical accuracy.

In spite of mixed findings and the problems inherent in these studies, it is hard not to think that personality has nothing to do with the success of second language learning. However, the relationship is complicated, and it is probably not ascribable to personality alone. Along with findings on personality characteristics, other factors such as motivation and language aptitude mentioned in this chapter will contribute to second language learning.

Willingness to Communicate

Embracing a social psychological tradition, anxiety has recently been studied under the wider construct of *willingness to communicate* (WTC). WTC refers to the predisposition towards talkativeness that learners have. Thus, it is the behavioral intent that can bring about actual communicative behavior (MacIntyre, Clément, Dörnyei, & Noels, 1998). ManIntyre et al. (1998) notes that learners who are willing to communicate in a wide range of conversational interactions are able to do so because "their prior language learning has led to development of self-confidence, which is based on a lack of anxiety combined with a sufficient level of communicative competence, arising from a series of reasonably pleasant [language learning] experiences" (p. 548). This also indicates that WTC addresses multiple dimensions of learners' experiences, including the psychological, linguistic, educational, and communicative (MacIntyre, Burns, & Jessome, 2011). This conception of WTC tells us that WTC is affected by a number of features, such as the immediate situation in which learners find themselves and the motivational propensities they have. For instance, in the second language classroom, learners' WTC may be influenced by the classroom interactional patterns, their interlocutors, as well as type and topic (Cao, 2011). As such, WTC varies: it can be high at times and low at others (MacIntyre et al., 2011).

Learning Strategies

It is commonly observed that not only are some language learners more successful than others, but good learners also sometimes do different things that other learners do not. In other words, some successful learners use their own strategies. Oxford (2011) defines learning strategies as "the learners' goal-directed actions for improving language proficiency or achievement, completing a task, or making learning more efficient, effective, and easier" (p. 167). For instance, in order to remember difficult words, learners may consciously choose to associate a particular new word with one they already know. If learners find making such association effective in remembering the new word, they will continue using this strategy.

Oxford (1990) proposes taxonomies of strategy use. In her work, Oxford classifies strategy use into direct strategies and indirect strategies. *Direct strategies* (i.e., strategies assumed to have a direct impact on learning) include memory strategies (e.g., creating mental linkages, applying images and sounds, employing action, and reviewing well), cognitive strategies (e.g., practicing, analyzing, note-taking, and summarizing), and compensation strategies (e.g., guessing intelligently and overcoming limitations in speaking and writing). *Indirect strategies* (i.e., strategies that indirectly support learning) are metacognitive strategies (e.g., arranging and planning learning and evaluating learning process and outcome), affective strategies (e.g., lowering anxiety and encouraging), and social strategies (e.g., asking questions, cooperating with others, and empathizing with others). Based on this conceptualization of strategic competence, Oxford develops the Strategy Inventory of Language Learning (SILL), which has been administered widely and adapted for use with different types of second language learners to increase their awareness of learning strategies.

Another well-known conceptualization of strategy use is proposed by O'Malley and Chamont (1990). They identify learning strategies in terms of metacognitive strategies, cognitive strategies, and socioaffective strategies. Metacognitive strategies are thinking actions designed to regulate learning and performances through planning, monitoring, and evaluating. Cognitive strategies include more specific learning tasks such as repetition, grouping, note-taking, deduction, transformation, and summarization. Socioaffective strategies are interpersonal and feeling strategies such as working with one or more people to obtain feedback or pool information.

Although the definitions and boundaries of learning strategies vary, learning strategies discussed in second language studies commonly include four strategies: cognitive strategies, metacognitive strategies, social strategies, and affective strategies. One issue surrounding learning strategies is whether or not they should be taught in classrooms. Some researchers suggest that strategy instruction can facilitate second language learning while some argue that class time is better spent providing learners with input and output opportunities. In spite of the ongoing debate over the necessity of strategy instruction, many educators and teachers based on their classroom teaching experiences point out that there are many language learners who are not capable of independently developing their own learning strategies and do not know how to study. In order to help those who are interested in strategy instruction, several researchers have proposed guidelines on how to teach strategies. For example, Dörnyei (2005) proposes the general goal of strategy instruction: increasing the learners' awareness and rationale for strategy use in second language learning, introducing learners to new strategies and modeling their use, giving learners opportunities to use strategies, and allowing them to share reflections about strategy effectiveness.

The following are some popular techniques used for teaching strategies to students:

> 1. Teacher modeling: Teachers show the cognitive, affective, and social process they use when approaching and carrying out a task by verbalizing these thoughts (i.e., think aloud).
> 2. Awareness raising: Teachers let students think about the strategies they used and how other strategies can help them to learn better. This can be done through teacher-led discussion, small-group sharing, and learning diaries.
> 3. Guided practice: Teachers provide students with a set of guidelines and activities which then lead to planning which strategies to use, monitoring the use of strategies, and evaluating the effectiveness of the strategies.
> 4. Review, reflect, and reuse: Students are asked to review and evaluate the way they use strategies, and this enables them to distinguish useful ones from ineffective ones.
>
> (Adapted from Goh, 2012, p. 73)

If strategy instruction can provide learners with guidelines for strategy use which can help them become better learners, there seems no reason to be against offering strategy instruction in classrooms.

89

Age

Undoubtedly, children are generally believed to be better at learning a second language than adults. This is reflected in what is known as the *Critical Period Hypothesis* (CPH) – animals, including human beings, are inherently programed to acquire certain types of knowledge and skills at specific times in life (Lenneberg, 1967). Indeed, the CPH was established based on several phenomena in animal behavior and first proposed to explain first language acquisition. It has been claimed that language acquisition will be incomplete or even impossible after puberty. It is difficult to find evidence that supports or rejects the CPH in first language acquisition since all children are naturally exposed to language at an early age. However, there is some evidence from research of tragic cases where children were deprived from contact with language and social interaction until the age of puberty. This was the case of Genie (Curtiss, 1977) and of several untamed children (discussed in Candland, 1993). Under such extremely detrimental circumstances, these adolescents could not learn their first language, and although a lot of efforts were made to teach them language after they were rescued, it was impossible for them to develop language to the level of their peers.

Additional evidence came from the studies about postponed first language acquisition in the deaf population (Mayberry & Lock, 2003; Newport, 1990). Unfortunately, about 90 per cent of deaf children who were born to hearing parents are not exposed to sign languages for the first six years of life;

thus, they learn no first language until they are sent to school. Newport (1990) compared deaf children who were exposed to American Sign Language (ASL) from birth (native signer) to children who started learning ASL between four and six years of age (early learners) and children who began learning ASL after age twelve (late learner). The research showed that native signers used grammar markers more consistently than early learners who used the markers more consistently than late learners. Similar findings were reported in another research with deaf children (Mayberry, 2007; Mayberry & Lock, 2003), and these studies provided evidence supporting the CPH in first language acquisition.

• Effects of Age on Second Language Learning

Then, the next logical question is whether or not the CPH functions in second language acquisition in the same way as it does in first language acquisition. Before discussing empirical research into the age effects on second language *ultimate attainment*, it appears necessary to mention an alternative term of the CPH used in the SLA – *sensitive period*. This is more gradual in its end point and allows for greater variation in attainment (Long, 1990). The CPH predicts there should be a dramatic drop-off, while the Sensitive Period Hypothesis predicts sensitivity, but not absolute drop-offs. The SPH implies that a learning decline might be gradual.

Some empirical studies into age and second language learning

People generally believe that individuals do not achieve

a native-like accent in a second language unless they are exposed to it at an early age, and such beliefs have been confirmed by numerous studies (e.g., Ramsey & Wright, 1974). However, some people argue that it is not necessarily true that adult learners cannot achieve native-like proficiency in phonology. For instance, Neufeld (1979) claimed that improved teaching techniques can improve learners' phonological proficiency in performing certain tasks. Although it would be possible for adult second language learners to perform like native-speakers by imitating native accents in a short task, no studies demonstrated a teaching technique successful enough to result in native-like pronunciation in everyday encounters. However, this does not necessarily mean that it is impossible for post-pubertal second language learners to achieve pronunciation which is not distinguishable from native speakers of the language. Several studies (Bongaerts, 1999; Ioup, Boustagui, El Tigi, & Moselle, 1994) found some exceptionally successful late second language learners who achieved native-like proficiency in the area of phonology.

What about other areas of the language? A great deal of research was carried out to investigate the effects of age on the area of second language morphosyntax. Building on the pioneering studies done by Oyama (1976) and Patkowski (1980), many studies examined whether or not age and morphosyntax attainment are systematically related. Ultimate attainment is generally measured by comparing second language learners' responses on grammaticality judgement tasks along differing arrival ages and against a native speaker baseline. For instance, in Johnson and Newport (1989), 46 Chinese and Korean speakers learning English who were college educated and had been living in the US for at least five years took a 276-item grammaticality judgement test. There was a significant negative correlation between age of arrival (ranged from 3 to 39) and grammaticality judgement score. However, the correlation was large only for the 3 to 16 age group and disappeared for the 17 to 39 group. While the youngest group who had arrived in the US between 3 to 7 years old performed like the native speaker, the adolescent group who had arrived between 8 and 16 years old scored linearly declining with age. In the case of the adult group who was between 17 to 39 years old when they arrived in the US scored erratically, showing no relationship between the age of arrival and the score of grammaticality judgement test. Unexpectedly, there was one learner who had arrived at age 23 scored 92 per cent of accuracy, as high as native speakers.

Birdsong and Molis (2001) replicated Johnson and Newport (1989) with a different first language group, 61 college-educated Spanish speakers of L2 English. Birdsong and Molis employed the same grammaticality judgement test Johnson and Newport used. The study reported that the early arrival group (between age 3 and 16) showed no variation and obtained near perfect scores. But, there was a significant negative correlation between the late arrivals and the test score. As found in Johnson and Newport (1989), there were also 13 late arrivals (17 years old or older when they arrived) who obtained 92 per cent or higher scores.

The outcome of Birdsong and Molis (2001) and Johnson and Newport (1989) look similar, especially, in that both studies reported a negative correlation between the age of arrival and grammaticality judgement test and found late arrivals who scored as high as native speakers. However, the studies differ when the results are examined in details. First, Johnson and Newport (1998) reported that only the early group who had arrived at a very early age (3 to 7 years old) achieved native-like proficiency and showed no relationship between the age and the test score. In the case of the adolescent group who was between 8 and 16, a significant negative relationship was found between the age and the score. In contrast, in Birdsong and Molis (2001), the learners who had arrived in the US at up to 16 years old not only achieved near perfect scores like native speakers, but also showed no individual variations. In other words, the so-called critical period in Johnson and Newport was 7 years old while the critical period in Birdsong and Moliswas 16. Put differently, the critical period in the studies was not congruent.

Bialystok (1997) argued against the critical period as a decisive factor in the success of second language learning. She looked into the acquisition of French gender marking by English and German speakers and found that age of onset of learning does not have significant effects. What seemed more relevant to the ultimate attainment is the length of the study (or the length of stay in the target community). Furthermore, based on a reanalysis of Johnson and Newport (1989) data, Bialystok and Hakuta (1994) found that not all structures were age-related. In other words, some structures were affected by the age of the onset of learning, but some were not.

In sum, young children are more likely to attain native-like proficiency in a second language compared to adolescents or adults, especially in the area of phonology. However, some exceptional cases of adult learners who achieved native-like proficiency have been reported. In addition, all structures are not equally related to the age of onset of second language learning. Therefore, in SLA, the critical period does not effectively explain the age-related phenomenon – there are multiple critical periods, not one single critical period. A critical period can differ across the part of language (e.g., phonology, morphosyntax, syntax, and pragmatics) and even within the same part of language.

Explanations for age-related phenomenon

If there is a critical period, at least a sensitive period, the next question is why this is the case. Various explanations have been suggested. A loss of the language learning faculty has been presented as an explanation (Birdsong, 1999). In addition, some people claim that neurological changes prevent adults from using their brains in the same way children do on language-learning tasks. As human beings age, progressive lateralization of brainy functions takes place, and as a result, the neural substrate needed for language learning is no longer fully available. This is usually presented as a loss of plasticity, or flexibility, in the brain. Cognitive factors are also considered in explaining the age-related phenomenon in SLA. Cognitive abilities adults possess may result in less successful learning compared to children. Furthermore, different social contexts adults and children are exposed to may need to be considered. Generally, children are exposed to better conditions for language learning such as getting more modified input and output opportunities through schooling. Needless to say, no single explanation can account for age-related differences.

We are still left with the question –"Is younger better?"

Children seem to have more favorable conditions both biologically and socially. However, it does not mean that early start guarantees the success of second language learning (Burstall, 1975). It is not uncommon to see that learners who have had an early start feel frustrated and demotivated by lack of progress. In addition, if early starters are not continually exposed to second language input, they will be caught by learners who start later but receive continuous exposure to second language. Undoubtedly, the age at which instruction begins is not the only determining variable of success in second language learning.

Chapter Concluding Remarks

If you consider your own second language experience or that of your friends, you will probably find some cases where the individual characteristics discussed in this chapter are associated with success or the lack of it in second language learning. However, it is not always easy to say that a certain element (e.g., motivation or personality) is exclusively related to the success of second language learning. This may be due to several reasons. One of them is that learner characteristics are not independent of one another. For instance, when an English learner says "I interact with native speakers very often," this can be interpreted in many different ways. This may be due to her outgoing personality, or this may be due to the fact that she is highly motivated. Or she is just surrounded by many English speakers. Furthermore, individual learners react differently in different conditions. For example, learners may consider themselves introverted when they are with unfamiliar people, but they may define themselves as extroverted when they are with friends. Measuring learner characteristics is sometimes problematic. Likewise, measuring learners' success in second language learning is not an easy task. To measure learning success, researchers need to define 'learning success' in second language learning. They will use different measurements depending on their definitions. If someone defines 'success' as 'having grammatical accuracy,' a grammar test will be used to measure 'learning success.' If someone sees 'success' as 'having communicative abilities,' an oral test will be used. Depending on the types of measurements used in research, a learner' learning success will be evaluated differently. Thus, the research into individual differences in second language learning requires careful interpretations. Nonetheless, the research shows that it is vital for a teacher to take learners' individual difference into account and to construct a learning environment in which more learners can be successful in learning a second language.

Chapter 3

Teaching Methods and Approaches

Chapter 3.

Teaching Methods and Approaches

Although second language acquisition theories account for how learners acquire non-primary languages, they do not explain how languages should be taught. Language teaching methods discussed in this chapter describe specific approaches for second language teaching. Many of the methods are built on second language acquisition theories, but some of them have a weak theoretical background. This chapter explains the history of methodological changes in second language teaching, focusing on major teaching methods.

101

Early Approaches to Language Teaching

• The Grammar-Translation Method

Prior to the twentieth century, a main purpose of learning a foreign language was to read literature written in Greek and Latin which were the lingua franca. Higher learning was carried out primarily in these languages all over Europe. In order to teach people to read literature in Greek and Latin, the grammar-translation approach was proposed and practiced widely in teaching Latin, but also of other languages as well. In the grammar-translation approach, as in the name of approach, learning grammar and practicing translation are key elements. Grammar instruction is given deductively (i.e., *deductive instruction*). In other words, grammar rule explanations are provided first and learners study about the forms and vocabulary in isolated context. Typically, teachers have learners read and translate target language texts into the mother tongue (or vice versa). Translation processes ensure that learners correctly understand the reading texts. Instruction is given in the native language. Obviously, the grammar-translation approach is better suited to developing reading skills rather than speaking skills – there is little use of the target language for communication. Thus, teachers do not have to be able to speak the target language fluently and it can be practiced in a large classroom. For these practical reasons, the grammar-translation approach is still used widely in many public schools around the world.

• **The Direct Method**

By the end of the nineteenth century, along with the development of public trasportation, people in Europe came to have opportunities to travel to other countries, and this made them have a desire to communicate with people there. As noted above, the grammar-translation approach is not useful for developing oral skills; therefore, a language teaching method for developing speaking skills was needed. Gouin proposed the direct method which put an emphasis on the ability to use rather than analyze a language. In the direct method, instruction is exclusively provided in the target language, and the use of the mother tongue is not permitted. Teachers use pictures, actions, and other materials to make meaning clear and comprehensible. Unlike the grammar-translation method, grammar is taught by repeated exposures to the target language in use, not through rules about forms (i.e., *inductive instruction*). Reading texts provides the content of instruction, but they are not analyzed grammatically. Since the method aims to develop learners' oral skills, the teacher is required to initiate a lot of questions and maintain conversations to elicit oral practices from learners. For this reason, the teacher must be a native speaker or have native-like proficiency in the target language. The essential element of the method is the exchanges of questions and answers between the teacher and students or among students, and a small size class is more suitable for this method.

- **The Audiolingual Approach**

The audiolingual approach was initiated from the Army Specialized Program established in 1942. As the name tells us, the program was created to train the United States army. As the US entered World War II, it was imperative for the US military to quickly teach the army foreign languages. The US government hired linguists to help teach languages and develop materials. In this context, the audiolingual method was established by Charles Fries (1945) trained in structural linguistics. Fries and his colleagues added features from both structural linguistics and behavior psychology. Thus, they believed that 'grammar' was the starting point of learning a language, and the structure of the language was identified with its distinctive sounds units, which then form lexical and grammatical elements, which then form higher structures such as phrases and clauses/sentences. Thus, the language is taught by intensive oral drilling of the basic sentence patterns. Since the primary focus of the method is on developing oral skills, the lesson is oral-based (i.e., dialogues) and mostly conducted in the target language. Memorization through repetition is emphasized and accurate pronunciation is stressed from the beginning. Grammar is taught inductively and it is sequenced and taught through planned exposure. Learners are only required to make oral production by memorizing the given dialogues. Teachers believe that learner errors should be stamped out before they become habits. Since the teacher only needs to be proficient in structures and learning materials and activities are controlled, he does not necessarily need to be fluent in the target language. This method is easily practiced in a large class.

More Recent Approaches to Language Teaching

• The Cognitive Approach

This approach was reaction to behaviorism, which had dominated psychology for several decades, under the influence of cognitive psychology. Cognitive psychologists asserted that stimulus-response conditioning could not account for all the complexities of human learning. In this approach, language learning is considered rule acquisition, not habit formation. In addition, the cognitive approach values *meaningful learning* over rote learning. Meaningful learning incorporates new information into "existing structures and memory systems, and the resulting associative links create stronger retention. Rote learning – taking in isolated bits and pieces of information that are not connected with one's existing cognitive structures – has little chance of creating long-term retention" (Brown, 2007, p. 65)

Some other features of the cognitive approach include that (a) grammar must be taught deductively and/or inductively, (b) new materials should be sequenced in such a way that they can be integrated with students' previous knowledge, and they should also be reviewed periodically (McLaughlin, 1987), (c) reading and writing are as important as listening and speaking, (d) students can benefit from instruction in language learning strategies, including metacognitive strategies that help them plan, organize, and monitor their learning (McLaughlin, 1987), and (e) errors are viewed as inevitable and used to enhance the learning process.

• The Affective-Humanistic Approach

This approach was developed as a reaction to the lack of consideration of learners' emotional factors in the previous teaching methods (Curran, 1972). It was also established based on the belief that language learners need to be prepared to communicate in the target language and live in the target community as members of the society. This approach attempts to remove barriers to language learning, making learners feel comfortable in the learning environments. Accordingly, it emphasizes the social climate in the classroom and the development of a positive relationship between the teacher and learners and among learners themselves. The focus in education shifts from teaching to learning; thus, the teacher is no longer the focal point in class but someone who facilitates learning processes. Language should be learner-centered, and learners' emotional attitude toward the target language and their own culture need to be considered. Celce-Murcia (2014) summarized the characteristics of the affective-humanistic approach as in the following: (a) the positive classroom atmosphere is considered more important than teaching materials and methods, (b) learners' feelings need to be respected, (c) communication which is meaningful for learners is vital, (d) peer support and interaction are viewed as essential for learning, and (e) the teacher is a facilitator who assists the process of learning and needs to be skillful in both the target language and the native language of learners.

• **The Comprehension Approach**

The comprehension approach, as the name suggests, places value on students' understanding the target language. This approach is based on the assumption that the process of second language acquisition is similar to the one of first language acquisition. As children develop listening skills before speaking skills, comprehension must precede production. This approach is most strongly associated with the linguists Winitz (1981) and Krashen (1982, 1983). The best-known of the comprehension approach is Krashen and Terrell's Natural Approach. One of the major characteristics is that it involves a silent period when learners attempt to assimilate the various meanings of the words that make up the target language. During the silent period, new language learners will try as much as possible to understand what the words mean and how to pronounce them. Thus, learners do not need to speak until they feel ready to do so. The key mechanism that brings about second language acquisition is comprehensible and meaningful input. Error correction is not seen as a necessary component in second language classrooms. The teacher should make input comprehensible using various teaching materials.

• **The Communicative Approach**

The communicative approach is based on the idea that learning language successfully comes through having to communicate real meaning. When learners are involved in real communication, their natural strategies for language acquisition

107

will be used, and this will lead them to learn to use the language. This is now used as an umbrella term for a number of teaching approaches, including communicative language teaching, content-based instruction, and task-based instruction. Although they have their own characteristics, they all share the following elements: (a) skills (i.e., listening, speaking, reading, and writing) are integrated from the beginning, (b) pair/group works are regularly used, (c) classroom activities and materials often consist of authentic tasks, and (d) the teacher's role is primarily facilitating communication and she should be able to use the target language fluently.

Communicative language teaching

The primary goal of this approach is for learners to develop communicative competence (Hymes, 1971), or communicative abilities. Simply put, its goal is to help learners become efficient language users in real-life situations; thus, it focuses on the functions language delivers (e.g., asking for information, asking for permission, etc.). Learners in this approach are encouraged to become involved in meaning-focused activities and this eventually results in language learning. Communicative language teaching (CLT) is not a method per se. There are no required specific content, syllabus, and teaching techniques. In other words, CLT can be employed in various ways. However, no matter how it is practiced in the classroom, it aims to cultivate communicative competence.

Communicative competence

Communicative competence is usually defined as the ability to interpret and enact appropriate social behaviors, and it entails the active participation of the learner in the production of the target language (Canale & Swain, 1980). It involves four types of competence, linguistic competence (grammatical competence), pragmatic competence (sociolinguistic competence), discourse competence, and strategic competence.

Linguistic competence is concerned with knowledge of the language itself, its form and meaning. More specifically, linguistic competence entails a knowledge of spelling, pronunciation, vocabulary, word formation, grammatical structure, and linguistic semantics. Færch, Haastrup, and Phillipson (1984) notes that "it is impossible to conceive of a person being communicatively competent without being linguistically competent" (p. 168). It has perhaps been a misunderstanding about CLT that it does not have to do with accuracy.

Pragmatic competence generally involves the ability to use language in order to achieve certain communicative goals and intentions. In order to do so, students need to learn about the relationship between grammatical forms and functions and how to use them differently in the given situations. For example, learners need to know the differences between the following two sentences:

> If you'd wait a minute, I will see if Mr. Kim is able to talk to you.
> Hang on a minute. I'll get him.

Both sentences convey the same function but they differ in terms of the degree of politeness and formality (i.e., register). For instance, the first sentence might be used by a young employee talking to his boss' wife while the second sentence

109

will be used by a man talking to his friend. The choices of sentence structures and vocabulary are determined by the relationships between interlocutors. Learners with pragmatic competence are able to use appropriate language depending on the social situations.

Discourse competence embraces a wide range of ability: how to initiate, maintain, and develop conversation, how to perform the turns in discourse, how to use cohesive devices in reading and writing text, and so on. In order to have a natural and successful conversation, people should have language strategies for initiating, entering, interrupting, checking, and confirming in conversation. For example, let's assume that a speaker wants to change a topic in conversation. In this case, some kinds of signals such as 'by the way' are needed. If he changes a topic without a signal, the conversation will become awkward. Using appropriate discourse markers help the conversation going smoothly. A similar kind of competence needs to be developed for writing and reading texts. To be effective readers and writers, second language learners should be able to understand and use proper discourse markers. For instance, in the sentence "Some wines have 'proprietary' names. That is to say, their names were created by the producers," the second sentence is a reformulation of the proposition in the first and offers an explanation. 'That is to say' links the meaning of the two. Discourse competence enables learners to create coherent texts or conversation.

Strategic competence refers to "how to cope in an authentic communicative situation and how to keep the communicative channel open" (Canale & Swain, 1980, p. 25). In other words, strategic competence has to do with using proper communication strategies when learners are unable to express what they want to say or understand what the interlocutor has said because of the lack of their second language resources. Consider the following conversation between a native speaker of English and a Korean student:

Example 3.1

Student:	My uncle has jeonwonjutak.
Native speaker:	What's that?
Student:	It's a house, not big, small, you know··· in the country. It has a garden··· (gestures a circle to show an area of surrounding land)··· you know.
Native speaker:	Oh, like a cottage, a country cottage.

The student does not know the word 'cottage' and she uses Korean. She code-switches to Korean first then paraphrase, assisted by gestures. In this example, she is trying to express what she wants to say by finding ways of compensating for her insecure knowledge of English.

The above episode only shows some examples of communication strategies which can be practiced in numerous other ways. Dörnyei (1995) lists the types of communication strategies as follows:

Avoidance strategies

1. Message abandonment: Leaving a message unfinished because of language difficulties
2. Topic avoidance: Avoiding topic areas or concepts that pose language difficulties.

Compensatory Strategies

1. Circumlocution: Describing or exemplifying the target object of

action (e.g., a small mat you put under a cup for a coaster)

2. Approximation: Using an alternative term which expresses the meaning of the target lexical item as closely as possible (e.g., birds for sparrows)
3. Use of all-purpose words: Extending a general, empty lexical item to contexts where specific words are lacking (e.g., thing and stuff)
4. Word coinage: Creating a non-existing L2 word based on a supposed rule (e.g., vegetarianist, firstly)
5. Prefabricated patterns: Using memorized stock phrases, usually for "survival" purposes (e.g., Where is the…?)
6. Nonlinguistic signals: Mime, gesture, facial expression, or sound imitation
7. Literal translation: Translating literally a lexical item, idiom, compound word, or structure from L1 to L2 (e.g., cow meat)
8. Foreignizing: Using a L1 word by adjusting it to L2 phonology (i.e., with a L2 pronunciation) and/or morphology (e.g., adding to it a L2 suffix)
9. Code-switching: Using a L1 word with L1 pronunciation
10. Appeal for help: Asking for aid from the interlocutor either directly (e.g., What do you call…?) or indirectly (e.g., rising intonation, pause, eye contact, puzzled expression)
11. Stalling or time-gaining strategies: Using fillers or hesitation devices to fill pauses and to gain time to think (e.g., well, now let's see, uh, as a matter of fact)

(Adapted from Dörnyei, 1995, p. 58)

Communication strategies are not limited to the strategies listed above. Any attempts learners make to keep communication going on are considered communication strategies. The ultimate aim of CLT is to help learners to become competent language users in real social contexts, and having proper communicative competence is essential to achieving this goal.

Content-based instruction

Content-based instruction (CBI) is fundamentally a curricular approach or framework, not a method. CBI is an approach to curriculum design that seeks to reach a balance between language and content instruction. This is not to say that there is never an emphasis on the language itself in CBI; on the contrary, CBI at its best integrates a focus on language into the context of content instruction. It has a "dual commitment to language- and content-learning objectives" (Stoller, 2004, p. 261). However, the curriculum is organized around content students will study, not around the linguistic syllabus. The basic assumption of CBI is that learners acquire the target language when they use it as a means of obtaining information, rather than as an end in it. The overall aim of CBI can be summarized as follows: (a) It helps learners construct knowledge and develop understandings about a topic and a learning task; (b) it encourages learners to use language meaningfully and purposefully; and (c) it enables learners to learn a language in the context of learning through language.

There are many things that can be considered 'content.' It depends on the chosen model. When CBI is employed as a main curriculum adopting immersion, sheltered, or adjunct models, school subject matters such as history and mathematics are the content that should be studied in class. However, in the case of the theme-based model, any current events, world cultures, or even general topics of interest are all valid 'content' options.

The CBI programs mentioned above reside on a continuum

ranging from programs that are content-driven to those that are language-driven. Immersion programs fall into the most content-driven approach, followed by sheltered programs and adjunct programs. Theme-based programs are classified as the most language-driven approach. In immersion programs, second language learners and native speakers are put into the same class, and the teacher teaches a subject matter and provides necessary assistance to the language learners. In sheltered programs, second language learners are separated from native speakers, and the teacher teaches a subject and she modifies her language to help them understand materials. The teacher's primary goal is for students to understand the content materials, but she also spends some time helping them with language-related issues (e.g., reading skills and vocabulary). In adjunct programs, students are enrolled in paired English and content classes (e.g., American history). Two separate instructors teach the classes, but they work together to coordinate their teaching objectives. For instance, the English teacher employs materials used in the subject class as content for the English language course. The instructional aims of these two classes differ: on the one hand, the content class focuses on helping students understand and learn the subject matter; on the other, the main goal of the English class is for students to improve their English skills. Through the support from the language class, students are able to learn the subject better. In theme-based programs, its primary focus is on language learning. The teacher uses a theme (e.g., cultural differences and aging well) as a point of departure for instruction in reading, listening, speaking, and writing skills.

Content-based classrooms may trigger learners' intrinsic

motivation and empowerment since they are focused on subject matter that is important for their lives. However, we are left with challenges, which ranges from developing a whole new genre of textbooks and materials to training teachers to teach both the language and the content.

Task-based instruction

In task-based language teaching (TBLT), lessons are constructed according to the language required to perform specific tasks rather than the aspects of language such as structures and vocabulary. Thus, in this approach, a task is considered as a unit of analysis and has to do with learners' needs in real-life. Simply put, a task is closely something learners do in real-life and task-based instruction brings such tasks into the classroom.

In order to understand the principles of task-based instruction, it is necessary to consider how tasks have been defined in second language literature. Skehan (1998) regards a task as an activity which satisfies the following criteria: "(a) Meaning is primary; (b) there is some communication problem to solve; (c) there is some sort of relationship to comparable real-world activities; (d) task completion has some priority; (e) the assessment of task performance is in terms of outcome" (p. 95).

Nunan (2005) makes a distinction between a real-world or target task (learners' uses of language in real life) and a pedagogic task (what learners do in class). Real-world tasks are designed to emphasize those skills that learners need to have so they can function in the real world; thus, these tasks are normally the final goal of a lesson or a unit. In contrast,

115

pedagogical tasks are intended as a connection between the classroom and the real world serving to prepare students for real-life language usage. Nunan (2005) defines a task as follows:

> A piece of classroom work that involves learners in comprehending, manipulating, producing or interacting in the target language while their attention is focused on mobilizing their grammatical knowledge in order to express meaning and in which the intention is to convey meaning rather than to manipulate form. The task should also have a sense of completeness, being able to stand alone as a communicative act in its own right with a beginning, middle and an end.
>
> (Nunan, 2005, p. 4)

According to Nunan, while engaging and completing a task, students will use previously learned information and incorporate it with new information they receive as they perform the task, and this eventually results in language learning. Connecting tasks to real-life situations enables learners to use language in a meaningful way and triggers learner motivation.

Employing real-life situations indicates the importance of acknowledging learner needs within the framework of TBLT. Different learners have different learning needs, and they may need to use the target language in different situations. For this reason, needs analysis not only informs the goal, but at the same time, it provides a direction to the construction of pedagogical activity in the classroom.

Some people argue that TBLT needs to be differentiated from *task-supported language teaching* (Ellis, 2003). It is important to note that, contrary to TBLT foundation, for which task is the unit of operation for both constructing the syllabus and for teaching, the use of tasks in task-supported language teaching is not the starting point. Task-supported language teaching primarily focuses on learning of language form, and tasks are allowed learners to practice specific forms in semi-authentic communication purposes (using structured communicative tasks).

Chapter Concluding Remarks

A teacher's approach to language teaching obviously underpins classroom teaching. As discussed in this chapter, there are many choices for teachers, and it is their decision which approach(es) they choose. Regardless of their choice, learners must be at the center of the teacher's decision. Learners' goals or needs, their level of proficiency, cognitive and emotional states, learning contexts and other related factors must be considered first. Ultimately, teachers can always use multiple approaches in designing and planning their courses and lessons.

117

Chapter 4

Teaching Listening

Chapter 4.

Teaching Listening

The importance of developing listening skills in second language was overlooked once it was considered that listening skills would be automatically developed as in first language acquisition. However, this changed as Krashen's (1983) ideas of comprehensible input and the ability to understand and participate in spoken communication gained prominence. Thereafter, the significance of listening skills has been emphasized in second language learning (Nunan, 1999). Listening is the crucial channel for language input and acquisition. We all know that without language input language acquisition cannot take place. Listening provides input, and without understanding input at the right level, learning cannot occur (Rost, 1994). In addition, in order to communicate effectively, listening comprehension skills are essential. This chapter includes essential theoretical explanations underlying the process of different types of listening and some practical guidelines teachers should know to develop listening instruction.

Process of Listening Comprehension: Top-down vs. Bottom-up Processes

In order to process and understand incoming speech, listeners are involved in a number of processes on multiple levels simultaneously. One of the well-known views on listening processing is the distinction between *top-down* and *bottom-up processes*. In the bottom-up part of the listening process, listeners decode the sounds "in a linear fashion, from the smallest meaningful units (or phonemes) to complete texts" (Nunan, 1999, p. 200). In other words, listeners decode phonemic units and link these to form words, link the words to form phrases, link the phrases to form utterances, and link the phrases to form complete meaningful texts.

In contrast, in top-down processing, listeners bring their existing knowledge, sometimes called 'inside the head' information, as opposed to the information that is available within the text itself. Using prior knowledge, listeners actively construct the meaning of the speaker using incoming sounds as clues. *Schema theory* provides theoretical underpinning of top-down processing. It is based on the concept that past experiences create mental agenda that helps people make sense of new experiences. Thus, learners' prior knowledge leads them to understand new information better.

Although bottom-up and top-down strategies are distinctive, they both are necessary to understand incoming spoken information effectively and accurately. In other words, interaction between bottom-up and top-down processing, so-called interactive processing, creates the most ideal conditions for comprehension. Thus, it is important for teachers to help learners employ both strategies when they process incoming information. If teachers suspect that there are gaps in their students' knowledge, the listening itself can be preceded by pre-activities which enable learners to effectively use bottom-up and top-down processing. Some of the exercises for bottom-up processing, top-down processing, and interactive processing are presented below:

Example 4.1: Bottom-up Processing Exercises

1. Goal: Differentiate between content and function words by stress pattern

   Read a series of sentences and predict which words will be stressed and which will be reduced. Listen to the sentences and confirm your predictions.

2. Goal: Recognize relevant details in the speech stream

   Listen to a short dialogue between a doctor and a nurse regarding changes in the daily schedule. Use an appointment chart. Cross out appointments that are being changed and write in new ones.

3. Goal: Identify specific points of information

   Read an outline of an interview between a reporter and an actor. The outline includes the main categories, but the specific examples are left blank. Listen to the interview and take notes on the information which belongs in the blanks.

Example 4.2: Top-down Processing Exercises

1. Goal: Listen to identify the speaker or the topic

   Listen to five short conversations and match each to a picture of the speakers and the settings.

2. Goal: Make inferences

Listen to a woman and a man ordering dinner in a restaurant. Based on the food choices they make, state which person is more conscious of health concerns.

3. Goal: Use the introduction to the lecture to predict its focus

 Listen to the introductory section of a lecture. Then, predict the topic of the lecture.

Example 4.3: Interactive Processing Exercises

1. Goal: Use word stress to understand the speaker's intent

 Listen to a series of statements about educational problems. In each statement, circle the words that are emphasized. With a partner, discuss what is important to the speaker and how the speaker feels about it.

2. Goal: Use context and knowledge of the world to build listening expectations; listen to confirm expectation

 Based on your knowledge of the US, predict what would happen to a Korean man who just emigrated from Korea to the States. Then listen to the man describe his experience and note what kinds of culture shock actually occurred. After listening, discuss with a partner whether your initial ideas are correct and how you have to revise your ideas based on your new knowledge.

Transactional and Interactional Languages

Brown and Yule (1983) divides language functions into language for transactional purposes and language for interactional purposes. *Transactional language* pertains messages focusing on content and carrying factual information.

124

It is used to offer instructions, explanations, descriptions, directions, and so on. Thus, the clarity and precision of the conveying message are significant. This type of talk dominates the classroom:

Example 4.4: Transactional Discourse

Teacher: now, here we have a substance in which heat is moving along the rod from a hot end to a cold end. Can anybody tell me the name we give to such a substance? A substance in which heat can flow? Nobody can tell me that? Well··· it's called a conductor. Anybody ever heard of that word before? Good, well··· I'll put it on the blackboard for you. It's called a conductor. What we are going to do today is have a look at some conductors.

(Adapted from Brown, Anderson, Shilcock, & Yule, 1984, p. 9)

In contrast, *interactional language* is person-oriented. While transactional language is viewed as business-type talk, interactional language is social-type talk. Therefore, the main purpose of interactional (interpersonal) language is creating and/or maintaining social relationships and its important features are those of identifying with other people's concerns and being agreeable to other people. One of the characteristics of interactional language is that it elicits agreement, hence the talk is about safe topics such as weather, travel, and so on (Brown & Levinson, 1978). In addition, there are often constant shifts of topic. See the following example:

Example 4.5: Interactional Discourse

A conversation between some people who have been talking about a couple who visit the area in the summer.

125

A: You know but erm…they used to go out in erm August, they used to come, you know the lovely sunsets you get, at that time and.

B: Oh, yes.

C: There's a nice new postcard. A nice – well I don't know how new it is, it's been a while since I've been here, of a sunset, a new one.

A: Oh that's a lovely one isn't it?

D: Yes, yes, it was in one of the calendars

A: Yes, that was last year's calendars it was on.

D: Was it last year's? It was on, it was John Forgan who took that one.

A: Yes, it's really lovely, this year's erm…the Anderson's house at Lenimore's in it, at erm… Thunder guy I should say.

D: They've sold their house.

A: Yes, the Andersons.

B: Oh, have they?

A: Yes, yes, erm…they weren't down last year at all.

(Adapted from Brown & Yule, 1983, pp. 11–12)

Like the example above, when the interactional discourse takes place between people who know each other and who share background knowledge about the topic that is being discussed, a great deal of details is left unspoken. Since the participants are able to fill out the details with their top-down comprehension, it is not necessary to elaborate on what is being discussed.

While the contrast between these two functions is usually clear, there are the cases where two functions are entangled. Nevertheless, when it comes to second language teaching, teachers need to provide experiences in both transactional and interactional talks since they differ not only in their purposes

126

but also in the types of discourses.

Classroom Instruction

• Selecting Listening Materials

When selecting listening materials, the teacher should consider whether they are related to students' needs and interests, whether they have authentic features, whether the level of task difficulty is suitable for learners, and whether they include various text types. Each one will be further discussed in this section.

Relevance

When teachers choose and develop listening lesson materials, first, they need to consider whether or not the listening lesson content and the outcome are relevant to the learner. This is crucial for getting and holding learner attention and triggering learner motivation. Relevance is easy to control when teachers create classroom listening materials. However, when teachers are required to use published materials, it is necessary to choose the lessons which are pertinent to their students. It may be necessary to modify the given materials according students' needs.

Authenticity

Using authentic data is also a vital issue in selecting listening materials. In many language classrooms, learners listen to and read materials created for language learners. Such materials are modified according to learner language proficiency; thus, they provide learners with security and comfort. However, it is also important to give learners opportunities to be exposed to authentic materials because non-authentic texts differ in certain ways from authentic texts. Non-authentic texts generally contain linguistic features more frequently used in written texts than spoken texts. For instance, they have few of the overlaps, hesitations, and false starts which are typical features of spoken language (Nunan, 1999). Hedge (2011) compares natural spontaneous talk with the language of audio recordings used in the class. Table 4.1 presents the differences.

TABLE 4.1

Differences between Authentic Talk and Scripted Talk

Authentic Talk	Scripted Talk
–variation in speed of delivery, often fast	–slow pace with little variation
–natural intonation	–exaggerated intonation patterns
–the natural features of connected speech, e.g., elision	–carefully articulated pronunciation
–variety of accents	–received pronunciation
–any grammatical structures natural to the topic	–regularly repeated structures
–colloquial language	–more formal language
–incomplete utterances	–complete utterances
–restructuring in longer, more complex sentences	–grammatically correct sentences
–speakers use ellipsis (e.g., miss out part of sentences)	–ellipsis infrequent (e.g., sentences usually complete)
–overlaps and interruption between speakers	–little overlap between speakers
–background noise present	–background noises absent

(Adapted from Hedge, 2011, p. 240)

128

Examples 4.6 and 4.7 presented below show how a scripted and an authentic dialogues are different:

Example 4.6: Scripted Dialogues (M = man, W = woman)

W: What type of exercise are you keen on?
M: I'm keen on running.
W: Do you do it regularly?
M: Er…. Three or four times a week.
W: Where do you run?
M: In the park.

Example 4. 7: Authentic Dialogue (M = man, W = woman, || means overlapping sentences)

M: Are you in, are you in fairly good shape? Do you still keep … keep fit?
W: [pause] I think so, yeah, In my opinion, yeah.
M: Well, what do you do exactly? To, to stay fit?
W: Mmm. Keep a routine, a routine like going… doing something every day.
M: Uh huh ||
W: || It doesn't matter what it is but
M: But ||
W: || What I do more is going to the gym, lifting weights || and
M: || Uh huh
W: (Wh…?)
M: But you do something, one of these, every day, one or two of these every day. Is it…?
W: No, I do it. I do it every day.
M: One or two of those every day, one or two of those exercises?
W: No, no, I do both of them || but
M: || Ah, right.
W: For example, when the gym is closed on ||

M: || Yeah

W: I do something every day. I have to do something every day.

M: Ah, right, right. OK.

(Adapted from Wilson, 2010, p. 31)

As presented in the examples, the authentic dialogue includes features such as overlapping sentences, repetitions, misunderstanding, false starts (like going … doing something), backchannel devices (uh huh), and ungrammatical forms (what I do more is…). In contrast, the scripted dialogue is well polished.

As noted before, modified listening material has its own benefits and purposes. It serves a pedagogical purpose by clearly modeling a grammar point (e.g., question forms and present simple) and expressions. However, the gap between authentic and non-authentic texts hinders learners from being prepared for dealing with real communication outside the classroom.

Task difficulty

Another important concern that should be considered in selecting listening materials is task difficulty. It is easy to think that grammatical complexity is the sole determining factor in task difficulty of listening materials, but there are other factors that make listening difficult. Anderson and Lynch (1988) suggests that (a) the organization of information (e.g., the information offered in the same way as it happens in real life is easier to understand than texts in which the items are presented out of order), (b) the familiarity of the topic, (c)

130

the explicitness and sufficiency of the information, and (d) the type of referring expressions used (e.g., use of pronouns rather than noun phrases makes texts more difficult) affect the difficulty of listening tasks. Nunan (1997) adds that difficulty is also affected by whether learners are asked to extract information directly from the text or if they are required to make an inference. The latter creates more difficult conditions than the former.

Brown (1995) also points out several factors that increase or decrease the ease of understanding: (a) the number of individuals (e.g., how many voices they hear) can affect the level of difficulty. More voices increase difficulty; (b) simple, specific spatial relationships are easier to understand than complex ones. For instance, in a recording giving directions, information like 'turn right at the bank' is easier to understand than 'go a little way on that street'; (c) events described according to the chronological order are easier to follow; (d) the number of inferences can shape the level of difficulty; and (e) the information consistent with what students already know is easier to understand. For instance, hearing someone talk about a movie they have seen is easier to understand than hearing the same type of conversation about one they have not seen.

The aforementioned factors will help the teacher choose the appropriate materials for students and adjust the level of task difficulty according to their proficiency. For instance, when the teacher needs to use a topic students are not familiar with, a short explanation of the topic can decrease the level of difficulty. If the material does not present the events chronologically, the teacher can give students some tips which can help them figure out the order of events to make the task easier.

Types of text features

As we listen to various types of spoken languages, teachers need to help learners work on a wide range of listening texts. Types of text features can be classified into monologues and dialogues. Monologues are nonreciprocal listening and involve listening to lectures, speeches, news, and public announcements. In contrast, dialogues are reciprocal listening like conversations; thus, in this case, learners become both speakers and listeners. Monologue speeches are usually pre-planned and scripted, so they are well organized and similar to written text with little repetition and rephrasing. In contrast, dialogues are usually unscripted, so they include features such as repetitions, rephrases, reformulations, and hesitations. In addition, contracted forms, incomplete sentences, fast pace, and colloquial expressions are often used.

• Using Three Stages of Listening

Effective listening activities aim to improve students' listening ability. One of the ways to achieve this goal is employing three stages of listening. Let's assume that we are asked to listen to something without knowing about what we will listen to and what we need to do during and after listening. This conditions will decrease our motivation to finish the task and increase the task difficulty. Three-stages-listening can help students be motivated and prepared for the given listening task.

132

Pre-listening stage

In this stage, the teacher needs to help learners 'tune in' to the listening texts, and this gives them a greater chance of success in a given task. One of the main goals of this stage is activating schemata. This can be done in various manners. For example, when learners do not have sufficient prior knowledge about the text they will listen to, they can receive background information and/or study some important grammar features and vocabulary in the listening texts. In addition, it is important to let students know a reason to listen. The pre-listening stage enables learners to comprehend the texts they will listen to in the following real-listening stage.

Activating schemata and predicting

One of the important tasks the teacher needs to carry out in the pre-stage is to help students activate schemata and predict what they are going to listen to based on their prior knowledge. There are various ways to do so. The easiest one is to have students free-write or talk about the topic they will listen to. This can be done individually, in pairs, or in groups. It could lead students to think about what they know and what they do not know about the topic. Using visual aids such as pictures, diagrams and realia (e.g., maps and brochures) can also trigger students' prior knowledge. In addition, a simple explanation about situations (e.g., answering the phone and ordering in a restaurant) is also useful. In addition, KWL charts can activate schemata and predict what they are going to listen to regarding a given topic. K stands for Know, W stands for Want to know, and L stands for Learn. Before listening, students can think about what they already know and what

133

they want to know about the topic. After listening, they can fill out the L part. If students do not have sufficient prior knowledge of a given topic, the teacher can provide reading texts. Additionally, the teacher can provide a list of key words from the listening passage, and this can help students not only to predict what will happen but also to decode the meaning while listening (i.e., bottom-up processing).

Establishing reasons for listening

Once students' schemata have been activated, the teacher needs to give them a purpose for listening. The purpose should be realistic and achievable. If the aim of listening is to write down every single word, it is not a reasonable goal. Setting questions beforehand is a good way of establishing a reason for listening. One of the easiest ways to make questions is to turn a title into a question. For instance, the title 'The Secrets to a Long Life' can be turned into 'What are the secrets to a long life?' Alternatively, students create as many questions as possible based on a given title and subheadings.

Things to avoid during the pre-listening stage

If the teacher uses the pre-listening stage effectively, students can be well prepared for the next stages. There are four things to avoid to make the pre-stage more useful (Wilson, 2010). First, teachers should not spend too much time in the pre-listening stage. Second, they should not give too much information to students. The idea of pre-stage is to introduce the topic rather than to give all the answers. Third, the pre-listening activity must be entirely relevant to what students will hear. Lastly, it is not a good strategy to use a listening activity as a pre-listening activity.

While-listening stage

This is the stage where learners actually listen to listening materials. While-listening activities ask students to show whether they understand or not. Students' understanding can be checked by having them produce something like note-taking, writing answers to questions, and completing charts, diagram, and sentences. Some activities only involve recognition responses such as answering multiple-choice and true-false questions, ticking words and phrases that are heard, and matching and choosing pictures. With recognition responses, students have less to do and therefore experience less distraction from listening. In contrast, with production responses, students are required to focus on other skills like grammar and spelling, and this may distract students from listening. It does not necessarily mean that recognition tasks are better than production tasks. Depending on students' listening ability, the teacher can decide which type of task is suitable for his students. For instance, for advanced learners who can handle both listening and writing simultaneously, production tasks will be appropriate, while production tasks will not be proper for beginning learners. Planning various ways of responses to the input will be further explained later.

One of the important practical questions the teacher needs to consider when asking students to listen for a passage is how many times they should listen. Some people may say 'once' since we may not have second and third chances in real life. Yes, it is true. However, for pedagogical purposes, giving students multiple opportunities to hear the input is sometimes necessary since it can reduce students' anxiety level. In addition, if a passage is difficult and long and/or if students need to focus on every details of the passage, re-listening is necessary. Based on the consideration of the pedagogical focus, student level, and the difficulty of a passage, the teacher needs to decide the number of re-listening opportunities.

Purposes of listening

In this stage, students are asked to listen for some purposes.

Listening for main idea

When we listen to something, we first need to grasp the overall intention of the speaker to understand the message. This is called listening for gist or main idea. In other words, understanding the main idea of text forms the basis of processing information. Gist exercises can be easily initiated by asking the questions like "What problem are they talking about?" "What is the lecture about?" and "What does the speaker think of the topic?"

Listening for specific information

While we are listening, we sometimes need to catch specific information ignoring what is not relevant to us. The skill of extracting the information we need requires an ability to ignore other irrelevant information. The following activities are useful to practice this skill:

Example 4.8: Date, Time, and Place

Students listen to a conversation between two friends. They are talking about an important school event which will be held next week. Students are asked to note down when and where the event is held while listening to the conversation.

136

Example 4.9: Spot the Difference

Students look at a picture and listen to a description of it. The description differs in many ways from the picture. Students are asked to identify the differences and mark them on the picture.

Listening for inference

Inferring is a thinking skill whereby we make inferences by going beyond what is actually said. Thus, inferring is closely related to schema theory. Indeed, to some extent, we often make inferences. For instance, when a friend says 'I took a book out of the library,' we infer that the speaker went to the library and checked out the book, using a library card or ID card although he did not mention how he got the book. It is obvious that everything is not stated explicitly, and there are times when we need to use inferring skills to make sense of what we are hearing. Here are two activities for practicing inferences:

Example 4.10: Pause and Prediction

The teacher pauses the recording frequently and asks students to anticipate what will happen next and why.

Example 4.11: Asking Inference Questions

The teacher makes a list of questions related to the recording. The answers for the questions are not explicitly stated in the passage. Students are required to make inferences to answer the questions.

Checking students' comprehension

Students' comprehension is not externally recognizable. We cannot peer into a student's brain and observe whether or

137

not he understands the incoming information. We can only infer what students have comprehended through their overt responses to the input. There are many different ways for the teacher to check students' comprehension:

Doing – the listener responds physically to a command (e.g., TPR)
Choosing – the listener selects from alternatives such as pictures and texts
Transferring – the listener draws a picture of what is heard
Answering – the listener answers questions about the message
Condensing – the listener outlines or takes notes on a lecture

These are some activities the teacher can use to encourage students to actively participate in the activities:

Example 4.12: Information Transfer

Students are asked to complete a drawing based on what they hear. For instance, students are asked to draw a pie chart of their partner's everyday schedule.

Example 4.14: Listen and Describe

The teacher tells a story but stops regularly and asks students the questions related to what he has just said. For example, the teacher says "I met a man with red hair and big hands" and then asks "What did he look like?"

Example 4.15: Note-taking

Note-taking can promote a higher level of attention. It forces students to extract the important points in a talk and lecture. Particularly, for language learners for academic purposes, note-taking is an important skill. For those who are not accustomed to taking a note, guided note-taking is useful. Compare two examples:

138

A. Listen to a lecture about Gustav Klimt and complete the notes.

Gustav Klimt was an Austrian symbolist painter

____

Klimt became one of the founding members and president of the Vienna Secession ________

Klimt's 'Golden Phase' was marked by positive critical reaction and financial success and __________________________

B. Listen to a lecture about Gustav Klimt and take notes under the headings.

Early life and education

Vienna Secession

Golden Phase

Both A and B provide some guides, but A is more specific and detailed. The teacher needs to decide how much of the guided information is needed according to students' ability.

Post-listening stage

In the post-listening stage, the first thing the teacher needs to do is checking the answers from the while-listening stage. By doing so, the teacher comes to know about problems students have, which will help him plan the next task or lesson. Besides checking the answers, there are other activities which are suitable for the post-listening stage such as discussion, critical responses, and information exchange. Here are some examples:

Example 4.16: Using Discussion Questions

The teacher provides a list of questions related to the topic of the listening passage. Alternatively, for advanced learners, the teacher lets them make discussion questions on their own in groups.

Example 4.17: Critical Responses

One of the most important features of a critical response to a listening passage is an understanding of the speaker's perspective. Then, the teacher needs to let students to decide whether they have the same view point or not. By helping students be critical, the teacher may use the questions that can lead them to find some features of bias and inconsistency:

- –Do you trust the speaker?
- –Could the speaker have said it differently? If so, how? Would this have changed the meaning?
- –What does the speaker's use of metaphor show us about his attitude to the topic?

Example 4.18: Information Exchange (Jigsaw)

One student listens to a recording of part of a story while a partner listens to another part. After listening, they share what they heard, and their combined knowledge allow them to put pieces together to make a complete story.

• Developing Listening Strategies

In order to become proficient listeners, learners need to develop listening strategies. Wilson (2010) introduces some ideas for teaching listening strategies. Table 4.2 presents what listening strategies learners need to develop, how to teach it, and when to teach it.

140

TABLE 4.2

Listening Strategy Instruction

Strategy	How to teach	When to teach
Use world knowledge to predict what will be said	–Before listening, discuss the subject. –Use KWL charts. –Have students predict what a passages is about based on the title/headline of it.	–Teach before students listen. –Additional texts such as news and lectures can be used to give students knowledge relevant to a given topic.
Use linguistic knowledge to predict what will be said	–Use fill–in–the–blanks exercise. –Students complete the exercise and check if their answers are correct while listening.	–Use this exercise before listening or after a first listening. –Teach collocations if possible.
Monitor performance while listening	–Pause regularly intervals during listening to check comprehension. –Ask questions (e.g., Who said X? What is the topic?).	–Use this during listening. –The strategy should be taught only occasionally as this interrupts the listening experience and can frustrate students. –This can be used with any listening texts but works better with extended texts.
Listening selectively and ignoring irrelevant details	–Give tasks that require listening for detail (e.g., train timetables and flight schedule). –Use fill–in–the–blanks exercise.	–Use this during listening. –Explain what students must listen for. –It can be reinforced during feedback in the post–listening stage.
Write down relevant information in shorthand	–Ask students to identify key words (the stressed words, which they should note) in full sentences. –Give students 'Who/Where/What/Why' charts. They take notes in the columns.	–The strategy requires pre–listening advice on what to note down and how to write it. –It requires extended feedback after listening, as students compare their notes.

Listen for key words for topic identification	–Ask students to listen again and pick out words. –Check with the script, if available.	–Teach this after the first listening.
Reconstruct orally or in writing	–Do dictogloss activities: tell a story several times. Students work together to reconstruct the story.	–The strategy is explained as the teacher gives the while–listening task.
Listen for transition points	–Teach linking devices (e.g., on the other hand, moreover, likewise, in conclusion etc.). –Pause a recording after the expression and ask students what comes next.	–The expressions need to be taught before listening. –The text can be paused during the second listening once students have got the main idea.
Ask for clarification	–Teach phrases such as 'Could you say that again?' 'What did you mean by XXX? –Give chances to students to use these expressions.	–The phrases need to be taught and practiced before listening. –The strategy requires face–to–face communication.

(Adapted from Wilson, 2010, pp. 35–37)

Some learners may be able to develop strategies on their own, but many of the students need some help from the teacher. The best way to teach strategies is to focus briefly on what needs to be taught and move on without overstressing the point: "Strategy training works best as a drip-feed process (little and often) rather than a flood" (Wilson, 2010, p. 37).

Chapter Concluding Remarks

In contrast to our first language listening ability, second language listening ability is not naturally developed. Rather, it needs to be taught and practiced, especially in English as a foreign language contexts. The listening process involves both overall top-down processing and bottom-up processing. Students can be prepared for dealing with incoming information using both processing interactively during the pre-listening stage in the classroom. In real-life, students are exposed to a variety of contexts. It can be transactional and interactional dialogues or it can be monologue speeches. It can be formal or informal situations. All of these tell us why the teacher needs to carefully design listening instruction including diverse listening texts, choosing materials suitable to students' level, and planning activities step-by-step. In addition, explicit instruction on listening strategies is effective to develop listening skills if it is practiced properly.

143

Chapter

5

Teaching Speaking

Chapter 5.

Teaching Speaking

When we ask someone if she has the ability to function in English, we use the question "Do you speak English?" In other words, speaking is viewed as the fundamental skill. However, speaking is an "activity requiring the integration of many subsystems" (Bailey & Savage, 1994, p. vi) and speaking in a second language has often been seen as the most challenging skill. As the function of communication in second language has been emphasized, developing speaking skills becomes a more significant task than ever in learning a second language.

Brown (2007) suggests several characteristics of speaking which make it difficult: (a) clustering (i.e., speech is segmented into thought groups rather than single words), (b) hesitation markers and pausing, (c) colloquial language features including idioms and slangs, and (d) suprasegmental features including stress, rhythm, and intonation. In addition, speaking almost always involves interaction with at least one other interlocutor; thus, learners are supposed to understand and monitor

147

other speaker(s) and make efforts to maintain the ongoing conversation. All these multiple demands are in place at the same time. This chapter discusses theoretical approaches to speaking instruction including different types of speaking events, foundations of competent second language speaking, and second language classroom implementations.

Different Types of Speaking Events

Speaking events can be classified in various ways (Thornbury, 2005). First, we can make a distinction between transactional and interpersonal functions according to the purpose of speaking. Transactional function aims to convey information and facilitate the changes of goods and services while interpersonal function has the purpose of initiating and maintaining relationships between people. In addition, speaking event can be characterized as either interactive (e.g., the conversation that takes place when we meet a friend) or non-interactive (e.g., leaving a message on a voice mailbox). Speaking event is also classified as planned (e.g., lectures) or unplanned. Using these distinctions, we can describe an event such as a conversation occurring between a student looking for a book and a staff in the library as a transactional, interactive, and unplanned speech. However, these distinctions are not absolute. The conversation can be both interpersonal and transactional as in the episodes below:

148

Example 5.1

Student:	Good morning.
Librarian:	Good morning. Nice weather.
Student:	Yes. How is your dog? Gets better?
Librarian:	A little bit. Are you looking for something?
Student:	Oh, yes. Do you know where this book is located?
Librarian:	Let me see. Oh, it's on the fourth floor. Use the elevator around the East Gate.

Example 5.2

Mother:	Morning, darling.
Daughter:	Good morning.
Mother:	Sleep well?
Daughter:	Well, not really. The thunder woke me up.
Mother:	Loud, wasn't it? Anyway, did your teacher tell you what the meeting is about?
Daughter:	Yes. You know Kathy… she was…

In the first example, the student asks the librarian how his dog is (interpersonal) and where a book is located (transitional). The mother, in the second example, asks whether the daughter slept well (interpersonal) and what the meeting is about (transactional). Our speech often carries out multiple functions.

The Foundation of Competent Second Language Speaking

Lazaraton (2014) suggests four factors that are essential for competent second language speaking: fluency, accuracy, appropriacy, and authenticity. Each one will be discussed below.

• Fluency and Accuracy

Edge and Garton (2009) defines *accuracy* as "conforming to the language system itself," while *fluency* is "operating the [language] system quickly" (p. 15). Fluency has to do with smoothness of language delivery. The next question that naturally comes to our mind is "Which one is more important than the other?" In the mid to late 1970s, some teachers put much more emphasis on fluency influenced by anti-grammar approach. Their arguments were based on the belief that language learners acquire their second language as they acquire the first language; thus, second language instruction needs to simulate the child's first language process (Krashen, 1983, elsewhere). However, many researchers found that fluency-oriented second language instruction was not enough for learners to be competent second language speakers (Lightbown & Spada, 1990; Long, 1996). It is now clear that fluency and accuracy are both important goals of second language instruction.

• Appropriacy

Appropriacy has to do with sociocultural context. Second language speakers should be able to be accurate and fluent, and they should also be able to communicate appropriately depending on who they are talking to, what they are talking about, and so on. Proper use of language in a given social situation is closely related to speech acts – "the ways in which people carry out specific social functions" (Ishihara & Cohen, 2010, p. 6) such as agreeing/disagreeing, asking for information, and introducing new events. Depending on social distance and social status among interlocutors, different language forms or discourse types need to be used to carry out the proper social functions of language (also called pragmatic appropiracy). Compare the examples below:

Example 5.3: Dialogue between a Husband and a Wife

Woman:	I'm home.
Man:	Got the medicine for Sarah?
Woman:	Here it is. And give her an extra calcium tablet.
Man:	Must we?
Woman:	Afraid so.

Example 5.4: Dialogue between a Pharmacist and a Customer

Woman:	Excuse me. I have a prescription for my daughter's arthritis.
Man:	Ok. It would be helpful if you gave her an extra calcium tablet every day.
Woman:	Do you think it is really necessary?
Man:	Yes, I am afraid it is.

The main messages delivered in both dialogues are similar, but the language forms and discourse types used are different from each other. In Example 5.3, the interlocutors have a very close relationship as a husband and a wife while, in Example 5.4, two people do not have any interpersonal relationship, so they use the language with formality. As the two dialogues show, depending on the interpersonal relationship we have with an interlocutor, the degree of formality (i.e., register) in language is decided. Thus, to be competent speakers, second language speakers should be able to choose the right form for the social situation they are in.

• Authenticity

Authenticity in second language learners' language is largely influenced by the language input they receive in the classroom. Using authentic materials in the classroom has long been discussed and no one disagrees on its importance and necessity. However, there have always been unsolved issues regarding this matter: How and how often should the teacher use authentic materials? Should the teacher use controlled simple sentences and activities for beginning learners and gradually introduce authentic materials and language use as proficiency level increases? Or should the teacher use authentic materials regardless of the level? The answers for these questions will vary; however, considering the fact that developing communication ability is strongly related to authentic language use and several studies point out the weaknesses of artificial materials, there is no reason for the teacher to put off students' exposure to authentic language uses. The teacher can bring various sources of authentic language to the classroom (e.g., newspapers, advertisements, etc.) Recently, with the advent of computer software for language data, the use of corpus-based second language instruction and conversation analysis has received attention.

Corpus-based second language instruction

Corpus is a large collection of naturally-occurring language text in a systematic way, and these large banks of language data become easily available and analyzed automatically using the appropriate software. In language education, corpus has been used for developing dictionaries with the computer-generated concordance output. This output shows how certain words and phrases are used in reality. In addition, the analysis informs us of the words or expressions frequently used in certain situations. This kind of information can be used when the teacher decides which words and expressions should be first introduced to learners. The analysis of corpus often shows the gap between the language examples presented in textbooks and the authentic use of language in real life. For instance, Shin and Nation (2008) analyzed the spoken data of the British National Corpus (BNC) to determine the top 100 expressions that would be most important for beginning second language learners. The result shows that 'I think' and 'You know' are by far the most prevalent collocations, while a greeting like 'good morning' are absent from the list of the top 100 expressions. Needless to say, this does not imply that frequency should be the only norm the teacher needs to ponder in syllabus or lesson design. There are other essential criteria such as learners' needs and proficiency level that should be considered and they have traditionally played an important role in deciding classroom syllabus. Employing corpus data in planning class activities, lessons, and syllabi will add more authenticity to the classroom instruction.

153

Conversation analysis

Lazaraton (2002) defines conversation analysis (CA) as "a sociological approach that attempts to uncover the systematic properties of sequential organization of talk and the social practices that are displayed by and embodied in talk-in-interaction" (p. 29). CA is related to the system that lies behind conversation and other forms of spoken language and it includes overall organization of conversation (e.g., openings, closings, transitions, and turn-taking), sequence structure (e.g., the linking of turns to the performance of actions), and repair (e.g., mechanisms for correcting problems of hearing and understanding in conversation). Wong and Warning (2010) proposes that "CA not only enriches our knowledge of what to teach, it also sharpens our understanding of how to teach" (p. 251). That is, knowledge of the interactional practices encoded in language can be used as instructional materials in the classroom. In addition, CA between the teacher and students provides important information about error correction, which will be discussed later in this chapter. CA shows not only how the teacher reacts to the students' errors but also how the students respond the teacher's reaction to their errors.

Classroom Instruction

• Accuracy-Oriented Tasks vs. Fluency-Oriented Tasks

In everyday usage, 'fluent' is often used interchangeably with

154

'proficient,' as in, "He's pretty fluent in English." However, we do not consider someone who speaks fluently but with many errors a proficient speaker. Conversely, someone who speaks haltingly but with a great deal of accuracy is not considered a proficient speaker. To be proficient speakers, we need to achieve both accuracy and fluency; yet, this is easier said than done. It is not feasible to help learners improve both accuracy and fluency simultaneously through one classroom activity. Below, two things will be mainly discussed: the characteristics of accuracy and fluency activities and some examples that can be easily employed in second language classrooms.

Accuracy-oriented activities

Accuracy-oriented activities (also called form-focused activities) force learners to use certain forms while they carry out the activities. Although the activity aims to develop learners' accurate use of the target language, in order to equip learners with the knowledge and skills needed for communication, the activity needs to be meaningful for students. Hedge (2011) proposes four characteristics which should be considered in designing meaningful accuracy-oriented activities: contextualized practice, personalizing language, building awareness of the social use of language, and building confidence.

> 1. Contextualized Practice
>
> Contextualized practice "aims to make clear the link between linguistic form and communicative function. This means finding a situation in which a structure is commonly used" (Hedge, 2011, p. 273). For example, to practice the present progressive form, a

phone conversation context can be useful (e.g., "Wait a minute. He's cleaning the garage"). Contextualization makes the practice meaningful and form-function mapping easy.

2. Personalizing Language

Personalizing language in activities involves students' expression of their own ideas, feelings, and preferences. Personalized practices trigger learner motivation and make the language more memorable as in the example below:

Example 5.5

Imagine that your friend is having trouble at work and is thinking of looking for another job. What would you say to your friend, using these expressions?

I (don't) think you ought to…
You should (shouldn't)…
It is (isn't) a good idea to…
It'd be better (not) to…
If I were you I would (wouldn't)…

3. Building Awareness of the Social Use of Language

This aims to attain "an understanding of what is appropriate social behavior and the language that accompanies it" (Hedge, 2011, p. 275). The attitude and language use which do not conform to social convention in certain situations (e.g., asking for information, closing a conversation, etc.) can be taken as an interpersonal offense rather than a language problem. Therefore, it is essential to inform students of proper language use for the given social context. The following activity is useful to teach such social convention:

Example 5.6: Closing Strategies

First, study the following expressions:

Ending conversations

Well, I suppose I ought to get on.
Listen, I really have to be going now.

Giving a reason for ending the conversation

I must get back to work.
I've got some work to do.
It's getting late.

Making arrangements to make contact again

(Look), we must get together some time.
(Listen), why don't we meet for lunch?
(Look), I'll give you a ring.

Leave-taking phrases

See you (soon/next···)
Good luck with/on···
Give my regards to···
Have a good evening/weekend/time on Monday
Take care.
Bye (for) now.

Now, in pairs, act out a telephone conversation with a friend who has been ill. Call your friend to tell her/him about a concert (or other events) you have been to. Say what it was like and if you enjoyed it. One of you must end the conversation. Say you have to go and give a good reason. Your friend must respond properly and make arrangements to meet at another time.

4. Building Confidence

By providing students with opportunities to repeat the expressions they are supposed to use in the activity, learners would feel that the activity is not difficult to carry out. This will help learners build confidence in using second language.

Fluency-oriented activities

Nation (2003) suggests that three conditions be provided for effective fluency activities: (a) all language items involved are already familiar to students, (b) the focus is on communication (not form) in real time, and (c) supports are in place for students to outperform their normal proficiency. Regarding the third condition, Goh (2007) puts forward three ways to support learners during fluency-oriented activities: language support, knowledge support, and strategy support. Language support includes the case where the teacher pre-teaches or reviews key expressions and structures prior to the activity. Knowledge support refers to the instances where the teacher offers background knowledge of the topic the activity deals with. Strategy support is concerned with using communication strategies, which can help students overcome the problems they may face during communication. These supports aim to reduce the cognitive load of students.

Bohlke (2014) also accounts for what should be considered in helping learners develop fluency: pre-task planning, task selection criteria, and task repetition.

> 1. Pre-task Planning
>
> The pre-task stage can help learners in many aspects. It can introduce new language, assist learners in shaping their ideas, activate schema, and recycle known language (Skehan, 1998). Planning time provides learners with an opportunity to attend to language areas not yet automatized (Goh, 2007), which eventually reduces the cognitive demands learners may experience during the activity.
>
> 2. Task Selection Criteria

Thornbury (2005) suggests some criteria the teacher should consider when they select fluency-based activities: interactivity, productivity, challenge, safety, purposefulness, and authenticity. First, an activity focusing on building fluency should be interactive such as discussion and role playing. In addition, an activity should require learners to use a wide amount of language to complete it. It should also be challenged; if an activity is too easy or difficult, they will be demotivated. At the same time, safety needs to be ensured. When learners carry out a challenging activity, they expect to take some risks, but they should be informed that taking a risk is part of learning process. In order to fulfill the criteria of purposefulness, the reason or outcome of an activity should be apparent to learners. Lastly, the teacher needs to choose or create activities that bear some resemblance to real-life language use (e.g., discussing something relevant to their lives).

3. Task Repetition

Another way to improve learner fluency is through task repetition. One of the difficulties learners face during a speaking activity is unpredictability. By repeating a task, learners are able to predict what will happen, and this lessens cognitive demands. Bygate (2001) claims that task repetition provides the foundation for learners to integrate their fluency, accuracy, and complexity.

Nation (2002), however, warns that task repetition can diminish an important element of fluency-oriented activities: "The more something is repeated, the less likely it will continue to be seen as a message-focused activity" (p. 270). He suggests that this problem can be compensated by balancing "the ease provided by the repetition against a challenge provided by new but similar material, reducing time, a new audience, and increasing complexity" (p. 270). Bohlke (2014) provides some examples of each solution:

159

(a) Reducing time

The teacher gives pairs one minute to perform a role play about shopping. The teacher then has the pairs repeat the role play, but this time in 45 seconds.

(b) A new audience

Students tell their group about an embarrassing moment, allowing listeners to ask questions. The students then tell the story again to a new group.

(c) New but similar material

A group agrees on a list of rules of the student cafeteria after they agree on a list of classroom rules.

(d) Increasing the complexity of the task

Groups have 50 dollars to spend for a class party that includes the teacher. The students decide how they will spend the money on food, drinks, and entertainment. The teacher then tells the groups that they only have 25 dollars, and the school director will also be attending.

(Adapted from Bohkle, 2014, p. 127)

Sample activities

Accuracy-oriented activities

In accuracy-oriented activities, learners' attention needs to be given to the forms such as how we use a new vocabulary item, construct a sentence, and pronounce a word. In order to do so, some aspects of the activities need to be controlled.

1. Drills

Drills are a type of language activity involving fixed patterns of teacher prompting and student responding as in the example below:

160

Example 5.7: Drills

Teacher: Where's Sue going? [holding up a picture of a supermarket] She is going to the supermarket.

Students: She is going to the supermarket.

Teacher: Where's Sue going? [holding up a picture of a post office]

Students: She is going to the post office.

This is an example of substitution drills. While students are engaged in this activity, they repeat the target form (i.e., be going to) with the given words (e.g., supermarket and post office). In other words, the language and content they need to use are controlled.

2. Information Transfer

Learners are asked to apply one mode (e.g., visual) to another (e.g., writing), which involves some transformation of the information. See the example below:

Example 5.8: Information Transfer

Teacher: Students, you have a diagram which explains the population of different cities in the USA. You will be asked to describe the diagram you have to the classmates. Look at the bottom of the paper. You nave the words and structures you need to use to describe the diagram. I will give you five minutes for preparation.

In this activity, the content is controlled and the language is also controlled to some extent. However, compared to Example 5.7, this is much less controlled in terms of the language form. Learners are able to practice the given words and structures through this activity.

Fluency-oriented activities

There are a wide range of fluency-based activities which can be used in the classroom. This section will introduce three typical types of activities: information-gap activities, role-play, and free discussion.

1. Information-gap Activities

We often ask someone for information we do not possess (e.g., ask someone on the street for directions). In other words, this type of activity creates authentic context. Along with this practical efficacy, from the theoretical point of view, information gap activities are beneficial for language acquisition since they generate the situation where negotiation of meaning can take place (Long, 1996, elsewhere). More specifically, there is a gap between the information the interlocutors possess, and in order to complete the activity, they need to find out the gap. See two typical types of gap activities below:

Example 5.9: Complete the Missing Information

In this type of information-gap activity, there is missing information and students have to work together to find the information. For instance, Student A has a map of a town and some stores and areas are already identified, but others are not. Student B has the same map, but the stores and areas that are already identified are different from those in the map Student A has. Student A and Student B are asked to find out the names of stores and areas which are missing from their maps. To complete this activity, they are required to ask for information they do not have and they deliver the information they do have.

Example 5.10: Find the Difference

In this type of activity, two students receive pictures that are similar but not identical. For example, Student A has a picture of Jenny's room before cleaning, and Student B has a picture of Jenny's room after cleaning. They have to find out the differences between the pictures.

Both activities require learners to exchange information they have, and they negotiate for meaning when they are not clear about the information they receive. Doughty and Pica (1986) reported that gap activities encouraged learners to understand each other through comprehension and confirmation checks and clarification requests more often than other types of activities.

2. Role-play

In this type of task, students simulate a real-world task in the classroom. A wide range of activities can be used from simple dialogues using specific information on role cards to more complex simulations. Regardless of the level of complexity, they all have in common in that the settings and roles are fixed by the teacher or materials. Using the target language in a given situation provides learners with a chance to develop sociolinguistic competence. In addition, simulating real life situation itself can trigger learner motivation.

3. Free Discussion

Free discussion activities provide learners with opportunities to talk about a wide range of topics which engage their interests, opinions, and experiences. One of the greatest advantages that free discussion activities have over other types of activities is that learners need to sustain conversation over a period of time and they naturally have a chance to practice the strategies required in interpersonal communication such as introducing a topic or changing a topic, taking and holding turns, and encouraging responses. As opposed to the benefits discussion activities have, many teachers worry about problems they often encounter in using this type of activity in the classroom. For example, it is

163

frequently observed that learners feel anxious when they are asked to talk about an unfamiliar topic. In addition, a few more confident, more extroverted, or more proficient learners often dominate the discussion. In order to avoid these possible problems, Hedge (2011) suggests some tips: (a) providing linguistic and/or content resources, (b) giving clear and careful instructions for each stage, (c) assigning a role to each member in a group, and (d) establishing clear goals for the discussion.

Balancing activities

It is important to find a balance between accuracy-oriented and fluency-oriented activities in planning a course. It has been claimed that, as students improve their language proficiency, increasing time should be allocated to fluency work (Brumfit, 1984). The assumption here is that beginning learners will need a strong focus on learning language forms through accuracy-oriented activities, and this may be true. However, it does not mean that fluency-oriented activities should not be employed for beginning learners. Furthermore, it does not necessarily imply that accuracy-oriented should be banned in the advanced class. It is easy to see that even learners who have sufficient confidence and ability to survive in the target language community have a lack of accuracy. In other words, even in highly advanced classes, accuracy-oriented activities can be used when learners need to focus on accuracy, or the teacher may draw learner attention to form during fluency-oriented activities by using correction strategies. Likewise, for beginners, fluency-oriented activities can be employed when they need opportunities to practice the resources they have learned in the situation which simulates real language use.

164

• Selecting Activity

Along with the matter of orientation of accuracy and fluency, there are some other characteristics the teacher should consider when they select activities to plan a class. Hedge (2011) suggests a list of criteria the teacher should ponder in selecting activities: (a) participation within the group (e.g., Does the activity ensure that all students co-operate and contribute, or does it allow some students to dominate?), (b) complexity of interaction (e.g., Does the group composition stay the same or does it change throughout the activity?), (c) opportunities for management of interaction (e.g., Do students need to manage topics and change topics?), (d) degree of simulation required (e.g., Does the activity keep students in the conversational setting of their own classroom or ask them to imagine another setting?), (e) structure of the activity (e.g., Is there a gap of some kind?), and (f) motivation (e.g., Is the topic one which will motivate a particular class?). Employing various types of activities can enhance different types of speaking ability; in addition, it is a way to provide proper activities to learners with different learning styles, intelligences, and language aptitude.

• Corrective Feedback in Teaching Speaking

The role of corrective feedback in second language learning has been debated over the last few decades. Some researchers, based on first language acquisition research, have argued that learners rarely take advantage of corrective feedback. The assumption here is that second language and first language are acquired through a similar process (Schwartz, 1993). However, a great deal of research evidence has revealed that second language learning, especially adult second language learning, differs from first language learning in many aspects (DeKeyser, 2000). In addition, it has been reported that second language learners prefer to receive correction of their errors (Kim & Han, 2007). In many foreign language situations, where there is little exposure to the target language or practice available in the community, corrective feedback is an expected role for the teacher. However, it seems necessary to bear in mind that teacher corrective feedback is not always beneficial for students. For example, Allwright (1988) points out that learners can be confused by teachers' inconsistent error correction:

Example 5.10

T:	When's your birthday, Alvaro?
Alvaro:	Twelfth November
T:	Okay. Now, Santos, when's your birthday?
Santos:	Fourteenth of September
T:	No. Listen: the fourteenth. Again···

(Allwright, 1998, p. 210)

In the above classroom conversation, the teacher does not correct Alvaro's error but corrects Santos' error of the same language point. This inconsistency may hinder learners from establishing a rule for the use of 'the.'

Error correction is a very complicated problem. When teachers offer corrective feedback, there are many different things to consider. The questions which have been raised in terms of error correction are (a) which error to correct; (b) when to correct the errors; (c) how to correct the errors. In the following section, these three crucial questions will be discussed.

Which error to correct

Correcting every single error learners make in the classroom is not possible, practical, or useful. In other words, the teacher needs to decide which error to correct. One of the criteria the teacher can use is whether a learner's incorrect utterance is systematic (i.e., systematic errors) or not (i.e., mistakes) (Corder, 1969). Systematic errors, also simply called *errors,* are evidence of a learner's current stage of interlanguage and show incomplete knowledge of the target language. With errors, the teacher needs to provide proper correction that can help learners to progress in their understanding of the target language. *Mistakes* are caused by an inability to perform that knowledge in production due to carelessness, distractions, tiredness, or other reasons. In the case of mistakes, learners can make self-correction when their attention is drawn to inaccurate utterances.

Another way of classifying errors is to decide whether or not errors hinder the flow of communication – global errors vs. local errors. Burt (1975) made a distinction between 'global' and 'local' errors. Global errors obstruct communication while local errors only affect a single element of a sentence, but do not prevent understanding between the interlocutors. For example, "There are long tress" can be easily understood by the listener as "tall trees" while "They ate smoked worm" is not easily adjusted to "They ate smoked eel." Hendrickson (1980) claims that global errors can be ignored. However, the learner's systematic errors (e.g., 'a news' and 'an advice') need to be corrected at some point, especially, when an activity focuses on accuracy. Determining what kind of errors should be corrected requires teachers' intuition and understanding of errors, activity types, and their students.

When to correct the errors

For this timing problem, teachers decide whether they will treat learners' errors immediately or later. This is largely determined by whether an activity learners are engaged in is fluency-oriented or accuracy-oriented. If the activity focuses on accuracy, the teacher immediately employs various ways to correct errors. However, in the case of fluency-oriented activities, delayed error correction is usually preferred: "During a fluency activity, it is generally accepted that the teacher should not interrupt students to point out a grammar or vocabulary error, or to correct pronunciation" (Lynch, 1997, p. 324). However, in some cases, the teacher intuitively feels that immediate corrective feedback is needed even during fluency-oriented activities. If this is the case, choosing an appropriate type of correction is important, and this will be discussed in the next section.

How to correct the errors

Corrective feedback can be delivered in various manners, and it can be largely classified into two types, direct correction or indirect correction. See the following examples:

Example 5.11 : Direct Correction

S: What means this word?

T: No, listen, what does this word mean?

Example 5.12: Indirect Correction

S: What means this word?

T: What does this word mean? Well, it is difficult to explain, but it means…

The examples above show the difference between direct correction and indirect correction: direct correction explicitly indicates that there is an error while indirect correction does implicitly. Although the question of which type of feedback is more effective than the other has been examined in many studies (Ellis, Loewen, & Erlam, 2006; Lyster & Saito, 2010), no conclusive findings have been reported. As a matter of fact, it may not be necessary to find out which one is better than the other because direct and indirect corrective feedback serve a different role, so they can be used for a different purpose: provision of direct corrective feedback is more appropriate during accuracy-oriented activities while indirect corrective feedback is more useful during fluency-oriented activities.

Whether the teacher offers correction immediately or not is closely related to the aim of an activity, and, generally, delayed corrective feedback is recommended during fluency-oriented activities. Immediate direct correction like Example 5.11 can interfere with the flow of communication. How about another type of immediate correction presented in Example 5.12? This is less likely to hinder the flow of communication than Example 5.11. In other words, it might be better not to restrict the time of provision of correction (e.g., immediate correction during accuracy-oriented activities and delayed correction during fluency-oriented). The teacher needs to be flexible in the choice of correction timing.

169

• Teaching Pronunciation

Pronunciation includes the role of individual sounds and suprasegmental features such as stress, rhythm, and intonation. Approaches to teaching pronunciation have changed considerably throughout the recent history of language teaching, moving from an emphasis on accurate production of individual sounds to focusing more on the broader, communicative aspects of connected speech such as intonation and stress. This transition reflects the increasing awareness of the communicative function of suprasegmental features in spoken discourse (Brown & Yule, 1983). Many studies have revealed the importance of suprasegmental features in intelligible speeches such as word stress and variations in pitch (Munro & Derwing, 2001). However, this does not mean that segmental issues can be totally ignored. The following sample lesson focuses on raising the awareness of the communicative function of suprasegmental features in spoken discourse. Example 5.13 leads students to be aware of the effect of a shifting tonic syllable on the meaning of an utterance.

Example 5.13: Three Little Words: Contrastive Stress

The teacher writes 'I love you' on the board, and asks the student which syllabus is stressed, eliciting that it is the word 'love.' He then writes up the same sentence twice. The students are asked to work in pairs to see if they can work out any other possible meanings by stressing the other words in the sentence. Suggested answers are as follows:

170

Sentences	Meaning
I **love** you.	I want you to know this.
I love **you.**	I don't love her. I love you.
I love you.	He doesn't, but I love you.

Perhaps the most critical aspect of pronunciation teaching materials is their widespread reliance on decontextualized language and lack of grounding in the reliance of actual communication. Pennington and Richards (1986) points out that it is "artificial to divorce pronunciation from communication and other aspects of language use" (p. 208). The following sample lessons show how pronunciation can be practiced in a communicative way.

Example 5.14: Collaborative Writing: Vowel Sounds

The teacher chooses a current problematic sound. Students are asked to write the lines of a poem, according to the following conditions: Some lines should start with a subject pronoun (I, you, he, she, it, etc.), and they should only use the past simple. The last word in each line should end with the sound being worked on. The lines are written on strips of paper, and the teacher collects the strips.

The following are random lines produced by an intermediate class who did this activity. In this example, the sound students work on is [iː]:

I wanted to be free.
He drank coffee.
This seat was not free.
He had a cup of tea.
I hurt my knee.
I sat under a tree.
I got stung by a bee.
Yesterday I lost my key.

171

Groups then select given lines and organize them into 'poems,' to be read out later to the class. The lines above were reorganized into the following:

Yesterday I lost my key.
I wanted to be free.
I sat under a tree.
I got stung by a bee.
I hurt my knee.

The task focuses students successfully on the sound in question. Students might also be given the chance to make the poem better.

Chapter Concluding Remarks

Speaking is a fundamental language skill, but it is not naturally developed in second language learning. As English is the lingua franca, the importance of communicative ability in English has become more emphasized than ever. To help students become competent English users in the globalization era, classroom instruction should employ balanced activities which can facilitate student development of both accuracy and fluency. In addition, the activities should ensure authenticity and practicality, so students are aware of the importance of different language uses in given contexts. The teacher also needs to let students to know that it takes time, efforts, and practice to develop speaking skills.

172

Chapter

6

Teaching Reading

Chapter 6.

Teaching Reading

In many second language teaching situations, reading has received special attention for many different reasons. One of the main reasons is that reading skill is considered central to obtain manifold information (e.g., current news and academic content). In addition, extensive exposure to linguistically comprehensible written texts can enhance language learning processes. In other words, reading skills are important not only for accessing content information but also for receiving linguistic resources. This chapter will discuss primary theories related to reading processes and practical techniques needed for classroom teaching implementation.

175

Reading Processes

In chapter 4, *bottom-up* and *top-down approaches* in the development of listening are discussed, and similar approaches are employed in relation to reading. In bottom-up processing, readers must first recognize letters, morphemes, syllabus, words, phrases, and sentences and use these linguistic data to derive meaning. A *phonics approach* to teaching reading supports a bottom-up approach, and it suggests that for readers to be successful they must be able to break a word down into its smallest parts, the individual sounds. Phonics is important, but it is not the main goal of teaching reading; bottom-up processing is a way, not the way, to understand written texts.

Reading also involves top-down processing, processing in which readers use their own intelligence and experience to understand a text. Readers use their background knowledge, make predictions, and search the text to confirm or reject the predictions. Thus, a passage can be understood even if all of the individual words are not understood. Goodman (1967) even calls reading a 'psycholinguistic guessing game.' A *whole language approach* to reading is supportive of a top-down approach of reading. Proponents of the whole language approach believe that language should not be broken down into letters and combinations of letters and 'decoded.' Instead, they believe that language is a complete system of making meaning, with words functioning in relation to each other in context.

One single approach, either bottom-up processing or top-down processing, cannot explain a comprehensive processing in which readers understand written texts. Many researchers have found that a combination of top-down and bottom-up processing, called interactive reading, is almost always a primary factor for successful teaching reading methodology.

Nuttall (1996) points out that "a reader continually shifts from one factor to another, now adopting a top-down approach to predict probable meaning, then move to a bottom-up approach to check whether that is really what the writer says" (p. 17). Murtagh (1989) further notes that the best second language readers are those who can "efficiently integrate" both bottom-up and top-down processes (p. 102).

Intensive Reading and Extensive Reading

Intensive reading as a methodology is a teacher centered approach. In this type of reading, the instructor directs most of what happens in class, including what to read, when to read, and what vocabulary, grammar, text organization or comprehension points are to be discussed. Students normally work with short texts with close guidance from the teacher. The aim of intensive reading is to help students obtain detailed meaning from the text, to develop reading skills, such as identifying main ideas and recognizing text connectors, and to enhance vocabulary and grammar knowledge. Brown (2007) sees intensive reading classes as a place where bottom-up and top-down processing are used interactively to achieve reading comprehension. In other words, attention should be given to phoneme and word recognition to progress toward meaning (bottom-up processing) as well as to the top-down processing.

Extensive reading, sometimes described as in opposition to intensive reading, is used for different purposes (Renandya & Jacobs, 2002). According to Carrell and Carson (1997), "extensive reading … generally involves rapid reading of large quantities of material or longer readings (e.g., whole books) for general understanding, with the focus generally on the meaning of what is being read than on the language" (pp. 49-50). In extensive reading, quantity of reading is emphasized, with attention given to student choice over reading materials. Hafiz and Tudor (1989) describes the aim of extensive reading:

> … to 'flood' learners with large quantities of L2 input with few or possibly no specific tasks to perform on this material. The pedagogical value attributed to extensive reading is based on the assumption that exposing learners to large quantities of meaningful and interesting L2 material will, in the long run, produce a beneficial effect on the learners' command of the L2.
>
> (Hafiz & Tudor, 1989, p. 5)

Priority is placed on fluency over accuracy, and on overall comprehension rather than detailed understanding of every word and syntactical structure. In order to make extensive reading more effective, reading materials available for learners should vary in terms of topic and genre, and learners need to be guided to choose materials within their level of

178

comprehension. In addition, learners are required to take part in post-reading activities (e.g., writing reflection). More importantly, the teacher should keep track of student progress (Renandya & Jacobs, 2002). However, extensive reading is generally more autonomous than the teacher-centered intensive reading approach, and puts the responsibility on students to monitor their own progress and strive to become life-long second language readers. Through extensive reading, they can develop reading skills and knowledge of the world and enhance language learning in such areas as spelling, vocabulary, grammar, and text structure. What is more, they come to realize that reading is enjoyable, and this helps them to have a positive attitude toward reading and develop a reading habit (Day & Bamford, 1998; Krashen, 2004). It is important to note that these two approaches to teaching reading – intensive and extensive reading – should not be seen as being in opposition to each other, as both serve different but complementary purposes.

Authenticity of Reading Materials

Traditionally, it has been assumed that language presented to learners should be simplified in some way to facilitate comprehension and learning. This can be true, but it should be remembered that simplification is not the only choice to facilitate learner comprehension. As a matter of fact, a simplified version can make a text more difficult to read than an original version because simplifying a text by changing the language often removes natural redundancy and makes the organization somewhat difficult for students to predict. Thus, the language learners are exposed to in the classroom is different from the one they will face in the real world. Simplified texts (or non-authentic texts) are useful for improving reading skills and preparing the learner for the eventual reading of real text. However, if the teacher only uses non-authentic and simplified texts for language teaching purposes, learners will not be equipped with the ability to deal with authentic texts outside the classroom.

Authentic texts are "real-life texts, not written for pedagogic purpose" (Wallace, 1992, p. 145). Authentic materials enable learners to interact with the real language and content rather than the form. Since learners deal with the language they need outside the classroom, they feel that they are learning a target language as it is used in the target language community, and this can trigger learner motivation and satisfy their needs. In addition, learners can be exposed to authentic cultural information and real language.

However, there are also some negative aspects to using authentic materials in the classroom. First, authentic texts can be too culturally biased, so learners often need a good knowledge of cultural background. Richards (2001) also notes that authentic materials often contain overly difficult language, unneeded vocabulary items, and complex language structures. If the wrong type of text is chosen, the vocabulary may not be relevant to the learner's needs and too many structures can create difficulty. This can eventually de-motivate learners.

Therefore, selecting authentic materials needs to be done

very carefully. The sources of authentic materials that can be used in the classroom are infinite– newspapers, magazines, TV programs, movies, songs, literature, and the Internet. When selecting materials from the various sources, the teacher needs to consider several conditions. Nuttall's (1996, 2000) three criteria, suitability, exploitability, and readability, provide a very useful guideline in selecting authentic texts.

According to Nuttall (2000), the most important criterion in selecting a reading textbook for students is the suitability of the content. In other words, the reading texts "should interest the readers – preferably enthrall and delight them" (p. 170). An interesting content should be accompanied by the criterion of exploitability. Nuttall (1996) defines it as the facilitation of learning – Does the passage allow the teacher to accomplish the objectives of the reading lesson? Exploitability can be decided based on the exercises and activities in the reading lesson. For instance, if one of the lesson objectives is to have learners discern the author's point of view, the passage should include the content which shows the author's attitude (e.g., opinions regarding a social issue). Reading passages which is basically descriptive is not appropriate for this type of activity. Lastly, readability refers to the surface features of a text in terms of structural and lexical complexity, which in fact affects readers' interests and responses to a text. As for structural constructions in a passage, if a passage contains grammatical constructions that learners do not know, they might have a hard time reading it. In addition, it is clear that as the number of unknown lexical items in a reading passage increases, the more difficult it is for students to read it with comprehension.

Classroom Instruction

• Developing and Utilizing Learners' Background Knowledge

A reader's background knowledge has a great influence on reading comprehension (Carrell & Connor, 1991), and this is also called schemata. According to schemata theory, "More information is contributed by the reader than by the print on the page" (Clarke & Silberstein, 1977, p. 136). Background knowledge includes all kinds of experiences that a reader brings to a text (e.g., life experience, educational experience, knowledge of topic, and cultural knowledge). The fact that learner schema affects reading comprehension can be interpreted to mean that reading comprehension can be enhanced by helping learners develop and utilize their background knowledge. Learners' background knowledge can be activated by asking questions and making predictions. In addition, they can develop background knowledge that is related to reading passages by using simple pre-reading activities. For example, if learners are reading about an unfamiliar topic, the teacher may need to introduce it beforehand. It can be done by simply explaining the topic or by providing visual aids (e.g., pictures or movies) related to the topic. In addition to such content schemata, formal schemata of texts help learner comprehension. Formal schemata refer to knowledge of the types of rhetorical organization in written texts (e.g., description, cause-effect, problem solution, and comparison). Formal schemata enable readers to predict the organization of the text, which makes reading easier.

• Selecting Proper Reading Materials

One of the most difficult tasks in teaching reading is choosing appropriate reading materials. There might be a number of things to be considered. As noted previously, authenticity is an important factor along with Nuttall's (1996, 2000) three criteria, suitability, exploitability, and readability. In addition to these conditions, learner interests and needs should be considered before any other criteria. Learner needs and interests very often go together: learners are interested in what they need and vice versa. Williams (1986) claims that "in the absence of interesting texts, very little is possible" (p. 42). Interest is important since it is closely related to motivation. When the topic of a passage is not of interest to students, their motivation to read is significantly diminished. In order to find readings that will interest students, teachers should try to find those that have a reasonable amount of new information since too much new information in a story makes it difficult to read, regardless of the interest level. In contrast, a passage that contains relatively little new information can be boring. As a means of examining learner interest, the teacher can use various approaches such as a ranking questionnaire and the teacher can also use an open-ended questionnaire.

Choosing reading texts appropriate for students' proficiency is also a key element for practicing effective reading instruction. The following questions may help the teacher check the relative ease or difficulty of a reading text for a particular purpose and a particular group of students:

- How is the information organized? Does the story line, narrative, or instruction follow familiar expectations? Are events are presented in natural chronological order? Are events and information presented following an obvious organization (main ideas first, details and examples second)?
- How familiar are students with the topic?
- Does the text contain redundancy? At the lower levels of proficiency, readers may find short, simple messages easier to process, but students with higher proficiency benefit from the natural redundancy of authentic language.
- Does the text offer visual support to aid in reading comprehension? Visual aids such as photographs, maps, and diagrams help students preview the content of the text, guess the meanings of unknown words, and check comprehension while reading.

Remember that the level of difficulty of a text is not the same as the level of difficulty of a reading task. The task itself may be difficult and challenging for students to perform, even when the reading text is easy to understand.

• Using Reading Aloud in the Classroom

While reading aloud, readers comprehend the meaning of the text by coordinating word recognition, comprehension, speaking, and pronunciation. This requires ability in highly complex ways. Students whose language skills are limited are not able to process at this level, and end up having to drop one or more of the elements. Usually the dropped element is comprehension, and reading aloud becomes simply pronouncing a series of words without regard for the meaning they carry individually and together. One way to use reading aloud productively in the language classroom is that the teacher demonstrates how to do it: the teacher reads aloud to the students as they follow along silently. The teacher uses inflection and tone to help them hear what the text is saying. Following along as the teacher reads will help students move from word-by-word reading to reading in phrases and thought units, as they do in their first language.Reading aloud can help learners develop their ability to simultaneously manage word recognition, comprehension, and speaking and pronunciation.

- **Working on Fluent Reading**

It can be easily seen in second language classrooms that even though language learners can read, much of their reading is not fluent, and that the teacher often overemphasizes accuracy that may impede fluency. However, developing the reading rate should not be ignored because we often face the situation where we must read accurately and quickly. In this regard, the teacher should prioritize helping readers reduce their reliance on a dictionary. Language learners often have the misconception that they need to know the meaning of every single word to understand reading passages. But, this is not true. Readers should spend more time analyzing and synthesizing the content of reading, not focusing on single words. Practicing *skimming* (reading for a main idea) and *scanning* (reading for specific information) skills and encouraging readers to guess what they do not know based on contextual clues are useful ways to improve fluency. In addition, repeated reading activity can be an effective way to develop fluency in reading.

• Teaching Reading Strategies

Reading strategies can be defined as "plans for solving problems encountered in constructing meaning" (Duffy, 1993, p. 232), ranging from bottom-up vocabulary strategies, such as guessing an unknown word based on the information given in the context, to more comprehensive actions, such as connecting what is being read to the reader's background knowledge. A great deal of research in first language and second language reading research has commonly shown that more proficient learners use various types of strategies in different ways while less proficient learners are limited in using reading strategies (Block, 1992; Jimenez, Garcia, & Pearson, 1995). Reading strategies can be taught to students, and strategies help improve student performance on comprehension and recall.

Strategies that can help students read more quickly and effectively include previewing, predicting, skimming and scanning, guessing from the text, and paraphrasing:

- Previewing: Previewing titles, section headings, and photo captions to get a sense of the structure and content of a reading text.

186

- Predicting: Using knowledge of the subject matter to make predictions about content and vocabulary and check comprehension; using knowledge of the text type and purpose to make predictions about discourse structure.
- Skimming and scanning: Using a quick survey of the text to get the main idea, identify text structure, confirm or question predictions.
- Guessing from context: Using prior knowledge of the subject and the ideas in the text as clues to the meanings of unknown words, instead of stopping to look them up; analyzing vocabulary; capitalizing discourse markers.
- Paraphrasing: Stopping at the end of a section to check comprehension by restating the information and ideas in the text.
- Distinguishing between literal and implied meaning: Using top-down processing skills and pragmatic information.

Instructors can help students learn when and how to use reading strategies in several ways. First, by using thinking aloud, the teacher can show learners the processes of previewing, predicting, skimming and scanning, and paraphrasing. In the following excerpt, a teacher uses the think-aloud technique to show what he is doing while reading:

> What I do first is read the title. I try to figure out what the passage is about. I look at the subheadings and pictures, too, if there are any. I ask myself what I know about the topic and what questions I have. Next, I read the first paragraph. I don't read every word, however, I let my eyes skim it very quickly – just picking out what I think are main ideas. I especially look at the content or meaning-bearing words – usually the nouns and verbs.
>
> (Adapted from Larsen-Freeman & Anderson, 2011, p. 182)

Second, the teacher uses class time for group and individual previewing and predicting activities as preparation for in-class or out-of-class reading. In addition, using fill-in-the-blank exercises to review vocabulary items helps students learn to guess meaning from context. Lastly, the teacher encourages learners to talk about what strategies they think will help them and talk after reading about what strategies they actually used. This helps students develop flexibility in their choice of strategies. By developing reading strategies, learners can realize that they can control their own reading experience, and they gain confidence in their ability to read the language.

• Implementing Three Stages of Reading

Reading should be planned, and three phases would be integrated into instructional sequence: pre-reading, while-reading, and post-reading.

Pre-reading stage

Pre-reading aims to prepare students for the assigned reading material, and a wide range of activities are possible at this stage. One of the first things the teacher should do is to motivate students by establishing a purpose for reading. In addition, the teacher can help learners become familiar with the reading content by reviewing own experiences in relation to the topic, activating learners' existing knowledge, and teaching key words and structures in the text. In this way the teacher can prepare them in terms of both schematic and language knowledge. Other possible activities include

188

talking about pictures accompanying the text, predicting from the title, and reading selected parts of the text in order to sample the ideas. Pre-reading activities are most important at lower levels of language proficiency and at earlier stages of reading instruction. As students become more proficient at using reading strategies, the teacher will be able to reduce the amount of guided pre-reading and allow students to do these activities by themselves.

While-reading stage

The while-reading stage is the actual reading of the text. During this stage readers should be making sense of the text and practice comprehension strategies (e.g., guessing unknown words based on contextual clues). At this stage, the teacher's responsibility is to help learners to understand the specific content and to provide guidance to ensure that learners comprehend the text. Such guidance can be supplied by activities which aims to encourage learners to be active as they read. Learners can be given activities which require them to make notes, confirm expectation, and predict the next part of the text from various clues. Other possible activities include giving learners questions to stop and thinking about, providing a chart for them to fill in with points of information, and having them complete an outline.

Post-reading stage

After every reading, there needs to be a post-reading activity in which the teacher further develops some of the ideas to reinforce the reading. Post-reading activities need to tie up with the reading purpose, so that learners make use of what they have read in a meaningful way. A range of activities are possible: comprehension questions, discussion, role-play, language-focused task (vocabulary or linguistic features), and writing.

Comprehension questions are one of the most commonly used type of post-reading activities. It is important for the teacher to employ different types of questions to check the level of learner understanding of the reading texts. Comprehension questions can be generally classified into three types – literal questions, inference questions, and evaluative questions. In the case of literal questions, the answers can be found in the text and they are directly stated (e.g., What is the main character's name?). Inferential questions require readers to find out information in between the lines or under the surface. Thus, the answers to the questions are not directly stated but implied in the text (e.g., Why did the main character shake her head? What do you think will happen next?). While the answers to literal and inference questions are found in the text directly or indirectly, the answers to evaluative questions require information outside of the text (e.g., How are you similar to the main character? Do you think the main character's decision is socially accepted?).

The following examples show various types of comprehension questions which can be used as while/post reading activities:

Example 6.1: Reading Passage & Comprehension Questions

The Hollywood sign in the hills that lines the northern border of Los Angeles is a famous landmark recognized the world over. The white-painted, 50-foot-high, sheet metal letters can be seen from great distances across the Los Angeles basin.

The sign was not constructed as one might suppose, by the movie business as a means of celebrating the importance of Hollywood to this industry; indeed, it was first constructed in 1923 as a means of advertising homes of sale in a 500-acre housing subdivision in a part of Los Angeles called "Hollywoodland." The sign that was constructed at the time, of course, said "Hollywoodland." Over the years, people began referring to the area by the shortened version "Hollywood," and after the sign and its site were donated to the city in 1945, the last four letters were removed.

The sign suffered from years of disrepair, and in 1973 it needed to be completely replaced, at a cost of $27,700 per letter. Various celebrities were instrumental in helping raise the needed funds. Rock star Alice Cooper, for example, bought an O in memory of Groucho Marx, and Hugh Hefner of Playboy famously held a benefit party to raise the money for the Y. The construction of the new sign was finally completed in 1978.

1. What is the topic of this passage?
    - (a) A famous sign
    - (b) A famous city
    - (c) World landmarks
    - (d) Hollywood versus Hollywoodland

2. The expression "the world over" in line 2 could best be replaced by
    - (a) in the norther parts of the world
    - (b) on top of the world
    - (c) in the entire world
    - (d) in the skies

3. It can be inferred from the passage that most people think that the Hollywood sign was first constructed by
   (a) an advertising company
   (b) the movie industry
   (c) a construction company
   (d) the city of Los Angeles

4. The pronoun "it" in line 5 refers to
   (a) the sign
   (b) the movie business
   (c) the importance of Hollywood
   (d) this industry

5. According to the passage, the Hollywood sign was first built in
   (a) 1923
   (b) 1949
   (c) 1973
   (d) 1978

6. Which of the following is NOT mentioned about Hollywoodland?
   (a) It used to be the name of an area of Los Angeles.
   (b) It was formerly the name on the sign in the hills.
   (c) There were houses for sale there.
   (d) It was the most expensive area of Los Angeles.

7. The passage indicates that the sign suffered because
   (a) people damaged it
   (b) it was not fixed
   (c) the weather was bad
   (d) it was poorly constructed

8. It can be inferred from the passage that the Hollywood sign was how old when it was necessary to replace it completely?
   (a) Ten years old

192

(b) Twenty-six years old

(c) Fifty years old

(d) Fifty-five years old

9. The word "replaced" in line 10 is closest in meaning to which of the following?

    (a) Moved to a new location

    (b) Destroyed

    (c) Found again

    (d) Exchanged for a newer one

10. According to the passage, how did celebrities help with the new sign?

    (a) They played instruments.

    (b) They raised the sign.

    (c) They helped get the money.

    (d) They took part in work parties to build the sign.

(Adapted from Phillips, 2001, pp. 421-422)

The questions ask a main idea (#1), expressions/idioms/phrases/vocabulary (#2 & #9), inferences (#3 & #8), grammatical features (#4), and details (scanning for a specifically stated details and supporting ideas, #5, #6, #7, & #10). The questions above represent a sample of TOEFL Test reading passages. Many of the questions are consistent with effective reading strategies such as skimming for main idea, scanning for details, guessing word meaning from context, and inferencing.

193

• Triggering Learner Motivation

Dörnyei's (2001a) process-oriented approach to motivation provides the teacher with a guide for what can be done in the classroom to initiate and maintain motivation. Borrowing Dörnyei's framework of motivational teaching practice, Anderson (2012) suggests motivational strategies to increase expected reward and decrease expected effort in second language reading instruction as in Table 6.1.

TABLE 6.1

Motivational Strategies to Increase Expected Reward and Decrease Expected Effort

Increasing Expected Reward	Decreasing Expected Effort
Creating the basic motivational conditions –Identify why reading is an important skill to develop –Discuss your passion for reading and the benefits of an avid reader	Creating the basic motivational conditions –Use pre–reading activity likes Shadow Reading to prepare students for meaningful engagement with a text. –Directly relate reading material to the previous knowledge of the readers to show them that what they are reading relates to things they have read and learned previously.
Generating initial motivation –Invite former students who are successful readers to your class and share how their improvements of reading skills has helped them reach their personal and academic goals. –Create class reading goals for words–per–minute and comprehension. Post the goals in the classroom.	Generating initial motivation –Engage the readers in specific reading rate improvement exercises so that they see that they can improve their reading fluency. –Use all of your knowledge about the specific group of students you are currently teaching to maintain achievable goals.

Maintaining and protecting motivation –Select a variety of reading passages at slightly different levels of difficulty so that students can see the progress they are making and the challenges that are still ahead to become better readers. –Model for your students the strategies that you use while reading in your second language.	Maintaining and protecting motivation –Allow readers to select some of their own reading materials for extensive reading outside the classroom. –Allow readers to work with their peers during comprehension checks.
Encouraging positive retrospective self–evaluation –Provide genuine praise for the improvement that students are making in increasing their reading fluency. –Establish the criteria for successful completion of reading texts prior to engaging in the reading.	Encouraging positive retrospective self–evaluation –Engage readers in comprehension checks that do not require them to take a written test. –Teach readers how to self–assess their performance based on predetermined criteria for successful completion of reading texts.

(Adapted from Anderson, 2012, p. 223)

As seen in the Table 6.1, reading instruction which focuses on developing learners' reading strategies and fluency and preparing learners for interactive processing (i.e., using both bottom-up and top-down processing) is eventually motivating learners to engage in reading. In addition, other tips suggested for developing reading instruction in this chapter, such as selecting proper reading materials and using pre-while-post reading stages, will promote learner motivation. This implies that well-planned effective reading instruction naturally motivates learners.

195

Chapter Concluding Remarks

With the growing emphasis on the role of language as a tool of communication, the importance of speaking and listening skills in the second language has been underlined. It is true that this tendency somewhat makes learners pay less attention to developing reading skills. However, as pointed out at the beginning of this chapter, reading skill is essential and vital not only for getting content information but also for receiving language input. Learners can be exposed to good quality and large quantity of input through reading, and this eventually helps learners develop second language ability, of course, including communication skills. The teacher needs to let students to recognize the power of reading in language learning and become invested in creating effective and interesting reading instruction based on the primary reading process theories and practical techniques discussed in this chapter.

Chapter 7

Teaching Writing

Chapter 7.

Teaching Writing

Learning to write in either a first or second language is one of the most challenging tasks. We can frequently see people who have poor command of writing in their first language and students who are struggling in writing classes even at university level. This tells us that learning to write well is a difficult and prolonged process for both first and second language learners. However, good writing skills are crucial not only for academic success but also for many other professions. In second language classrooms, writing is also used as a means of language learning, and will likely continue to occupy an important role in the school curriculum. This chapter focuses on the unique features of written language, theoretical and practical issues closely related to writing instruction, and tips for developing writing classes.

199

Differences between Written and Spoken Languages

One of the reasons learners feel challenged when learning to write is due to the differences between spoken and written languages. Although some forms of writing are closer to speech than others, it is generally accepted that the two are different in many ways.

First of all, while writing is usually permanent and written texts cannot usually be changed once they are written, speakers can correct themselves and change their utterances as they go along. Writing allows people to communicate across time and space as long as they share a language, while speech is usually used for immediate interactions. This tells us why written language needs to be explicit and clear. Writers receive no immediate feedback from their readers, except in computer-based communication. Therefore, they cannot rely on context to clarify things, so there is more need to explain things clearly and unambiguously than in speech, except in written correspondence between people who know one another well. In contrast, speech is usually a dynamic interaction between two or more people. Context and shared knowledge play a major role, so it is possible to leave much unsaid or indirectly implied. In addition, written texts are usually well organized and formulated since writers have time to plan and edit the texts before making the texts available for reading. Thus, written language tends to be more complex and intricate than speech with longer sentences and many subordinate clauses. In contrast, speakers are improvising as they speak. Spoken language tends to be full of repetitions, incomplete sentences, corrections, and interruptions, with the exception of formal speeches and other scripted forms of speech, such as news reports.

Genres and Register

The term genres is used to describe categories of written texts that have recognizable patterns, syntax, techniques, and/or conventions (e.g., essay and letters). There is a range of writing genres such as fiction, non-fiction, emails, letters, and essay. Each genre can be further classified into subgroups. For instance, fiction includes classic fiction, drama, comedy, and so on, and essay has a variety of types like descriptive essay and argumentative essay. We refer to the specific choice of vocabulary within genres as the *register* that the text is written in. Register differs across genres (e.g., the choice of sentence and vocabulary in essay and letters) and across subgenres (e.g., persuasive essay vs. narrative essay and formal letter vs. informal letter). Knowledge of different types of genres and the register is key for the writer to express ideas appropriately.

201

Formal Writing and Informal Writing

Formal writing and informal writing differ in many aspects. A formal text follows standard grammar rules and formal vocabulary, and is explicit. Little shared knowledge is taken for granted. In contrast, in informal writing, the text may not use formally correct grammar and standard vocabulary (e.g., using colloquial vocabulary such as 'yeah' for 'yes' and contracted forms like 'you'd'). The text usually targets a specific reader the writer personally knows; therefore, it may be largely implicit and there will be ellipses, assuming that the writer and audience have shared knowledge. In teaching, it is crucial to make students aware of the differences between the contexts and help them use appropriate writing in each situation.

Product-Oriented vs. Process-Oriented Writing

A *product-oriented approach* is a traditional approach to writing and focuses exclusively on correct grammar, composing practice, using the conventions of layout correctly (e.g., letters), and spelling. In product-oriented approach, the goal of writing in class is to teach students the patterns and forms of organization used in different kinds of written texts (e.g., differences between descriptive, narrative, expository, and persuasive writing; formats used to present information in an essay; different ways of organizing information in paragraphs). Thus, in this approach, students are supplied with a model text and study the highlighted features of the genre: "students are encouraged to mimic a model text, usually presented and analyzed at an early stage" (Gabrielatos, 2002, p. 5). In addition, students study the *rhetorical patterns* and grammatical rules used in different kinds of texts presented in model texts using controlled practices. For example, if they study a formal letter, they are asked to practice the language used to make formal requests (e.g., I would be grateful if you would…). Since people who favor this approach believe that correct sentence structure is an essential component: grammatical skills are emphasized, and errors in writing are avoided by asking students follow the given model text. In this approach, instead of allowing students freedom to create their own composition, controlled writing and guided writing are used. In sum, product-oriented writing focuses on ends, emphasizing the form and structures of writing rather than how writers create writing. The limitation of product-oriented writing is aptly pointed out by Murray (1980): "Process cannot be inferred from product any more than a pig can be inferred from a sausage" (p. 3).

In contrast, *process-oriented approaches* concern the process of how ideas are developed and formulated in writing. Process-oriented writing is connected with the sub-skills that fluent writers use when they compose: "many good writers employ a recursive, non-linear approach – writing of a draft may be interrupted by more planning, and revision may lead to reformulation, with a great deal of recycling to earlier stages" (Krashen, 1984, p. 17). In sum, student writers engage in their

203

writing tasks through a cyclical approach rather than a single-shot approach. They are expected to produce and submit complete and polished writing assignments by going through stages of drafting and receiving feedback on their drafts (e.g., feedback from peers and/or from the teacher) followed by revision (Kroll, 2001). Writing is considered as the result of a long and laborious process in which writers address several questions such as "what do I write about?" and "who is my audience?"

Product-oriented and process-oriented approaches differ in many aspects as explained above. However, it does not mean that a teacher should prefer one over the other. Both approaches are significant in teaching writing in second language classrooms. Product-oriented approach can help learners develop writing competence required for different forms of texts. Process-oriented approach will help learners organize their own thoughts in a systematic way. It has been claimed that the blending of the product and process approaches to teaching writing will assist student writers expanding their skills in using the language by experiencing a whole writing process as well as gaining knowledge from the model texts (Ferris, 2010).

Coherences and Cohesion

Coherence and *cohesion* are terms used in discourse analysis and text linguistics to describe the properties of written texts.

Coherence means the connection of ideas at the idea level, and cohesion means the connection of ideas at the sentence level. Since both are fundamental requirements for expressing writers' ideas in a logical way, a writing teacher needs to help students understand the concepts of coherence and cohesion.

Coherence is a quality of a piece of text that makes it meaningful in the minds of the readers. When a text is coherent, readers can follow and understand a text easily and understand the writer's purpose and line of thought. Coherence can be achieved by the way in which a writer sequences information. According to Canale (1982), for a text to have coherence, four conditions should be satisfied. First, presentation of ideas must be well organized and convey a sense of direction (i.e., development). Second, there must be consistency of facts, opinions, and writer perspective. Newly addressed ideas must be relevant to previously mentioned ideas (i.e., continuity). Third, main and supportive ideas must be accorded each idea (i.e., balance). Lastly, the ideas must be delivered by a thorough discourse (i.e., completeness). Coherence is also closely related to the issue of different genres (e.g., narratives, instructions, reports, and business letters) since every type of writing reflects a particular kind of text or discourse structure, and writers need to draw on these patterns in organizing their writing. One of the practical tools that can help improve the coherence of student writing is to use a reverse outline by having students make an outline of their papers after they have finished writing topic sentences. In this way, students can check whether the topic sentences are connected to the thesis statement of their paper and each paragraph is well sequenced. This may help students become more aware of how to develop their arguments effectively and coherently.

Cohesion refers to the grammatical and lexical linking within a text or sentence that holds a text together and gives it meaning. Establishing connections between sentences, sections, and even paragraphs using synonyms, adverbials, conjunctions, etc. creates cohesion in a text. Halliday and Hasan (1976) suggests that cohesion is attained by the use of a variety of lexical and grammatical relationships within sentences in the text and identify five sorts of cohesive ties: reference, substitution, ellipsis, conjunction, and lexical:

1. Reference: The students wanted to play more outside because they did not want to study.
2. Substitution: She has a lot of dolls but bought some French ones.
3. Ellipsis: Would you like to hear another song? I know two (songs) more.
4. Conjunction: He only had little time for the project. Nevertheless, he successfully finished it.
5. Lexical: "Which dress do you want to wear?" "I want my green dress."

Proper use of cohesive devices support the overall coherence. We can say that coherence is the macro level of text structure and cohesion is the micro level of syntax and vocabulary. Both these dimensions play an important role in clearly and effectively expressing the writer's thoughts.

206

Classroom Instruction

• Balancing Product-Oriented and Process-Oriented Approaches

Both product-oriented and process-oriented approaches have their own benefits and drawbacks; accordingly, complementary use of both approaches helps student writers develop their skills in using language by experiencing a whole writing process as well as gaining knowledge from the model texts. Such a complementary use of both approaches would help students to be authors rather than copiers, and so has the potential benefit of integrating critical thinking to their academic writing.

• Using Process-Oriented Writing to Teach Writing Process

Process-oriented writing as a classroom activity consists of four basic writing stages – planning, drafting, revising, and editing. Between the drafting and revising stages, students have a chance to get feedback from the teacher and/or peers. After finishing editing, students' final drafts are evaluated. Each stage and activity examples are described as follows.

Planning (pre-writing)

Pre-writing involves finding a topic, finding ideas about the topic, thinking about the topic, developing and organizing the ideas, and considering the purpose of the writing task and audience. At this stage, activities such as brainstorming, clustering (i.e., begin with a key word, then add other words, using association), conducting outside research, free writing, generating 'wh-' questions about a topic (teacher/student-initiated probes), discussing a topic or questions, and outlining can be useful to help learners to plan their writing tasks. In the classroom, these activities can be conducted individually or collectively. The following examples show ways of generating ideas:

Example 7.1: Planning Activities

Small group – The teacher asks students to get into groups and quickly produce ideas related to a given topic (e.g., talk about five things that should be considered in making an advertisement). Small groups can lead students to make ideas which the individual student can then use in their own planning.

Group feedback – Students think about a topic individually and then discuss it in pairs and then in groups. In this way, they can get feedback from others and expand their initial ideas.

Brainstorming – Students randomly write down words and phrases they have in mind in relation to a topic. Then, they make connections between the words and phrases, and they start to see patterns emerging and then organize their thoughts into sub-topics and categories.

Drafting

Once sufficient ideas are generated and organized at the planning stage, students put the ideas on paper. At the first drafting stage, students are encouraged to focus on the fluency

208

of writing without paying too much attention to grammatical accuracy or the neatness of the draft. Like at the planning stage, both collaborating and individual writing are possible.

Feedback

Feedback to student writing by the teacher or by peers is crucial in the successful implementation of process-oriented writing. Feedback is the teacher's quick reaction to students' drafts before they proceed to revise. Brown (2007) suggests that the teacher's feedback to the students' first draft should focus on general structural organization, the clarity of the overall thesis, major grammatical errors, and coherence between sentences and paragraphs. The teacher should resist the temptation to correct minor grammatical errors and to rewrite a student's sentence. The teacher's feedback to the subsequent drafts can include minor grammatical errors and specific comments on argument and logic.

Peer feedback can be carried out by having students respond to each other's writing in small groups or in pairs, and using a checklist (see below) can be helpful:.

- What is the greatest strength of this composition?
- What is the greatest weakness?
- What is the central idea of this composition?
- What are the ideas which need more elaboration?
- Where should more details or examples be added? Why?
- What are some of the questions that the writer has not answered?
- At which point does this composition fail to hold the reader's interest? Why?
- Where is the organization confusing?

209

- Where is the writing unclear or vague?

(Adapted from Reinking, Hart, & von der Osten, 2002, p. 52)

Revising

This is the stage where students incorporate the feedback into their writing, not just copying feedback. They reconsider what was written to examine how effectively they delivered their ideas to the reader. Revising is not merely checking for grammar errors. Students need to focus on the improvement of global content and the organization of ideas in the first revision stage.

Editing

At this stage, students edit their work for grammar, spelling, punctuation, wording, sentence structure and so on. Using a simple check list will guide students to check some of the common surface errors they usually make:

- Have you used your verbs in the correct tense?
- Are the verb forms correct?
- Have you checked for subject–verb agreement?
- Have you used the correct prepositions?
- Have you left out the articles where they are required?
- Have you used all your pronouns correctly?

(Adapted from Seow, 2008, p. 318)

Evaluating

Students' writing can be evaluated analytically (i.e., based on specific aspects of writing ability) or holistically (i.e., based on a global interpretation of the effectiveness of that piece of writing) (see Example 7.2 and Example 7.3). Students need to be informed of the criteria of evaluation in advance. Self-evaluation and peer-evaluation may be encouraged at this stage once they have been properly taught how to do it.

Example 7.2 Holistic Scoring Rubric (persuasive writing)

Score	Description
1	Little or no evidence of the skill –Inappropriate language for the intended audience –Few or no supporting arguments –Details lacking or irrelevant
3	Competent performance –Clear and appropriate language for the intended audience –Most supporting arguments are plausible and relevant –More details are relevant –Evidence of some innovative thinking
5	Outstanding performance –Clear, interesting, and appropriate language –Many plausible and relevant supporting argument –Ideas are creative and well–expressed

Example 7.3: Analytic Scoring Rubric

Organization –Adequate title, introduction, and conclusion –Appropriate use of transitional expression –Proper supporting evidence –Coherence and cohesion between sentences/paragraphs –Logical and complete conclusion	 5 5 10 5 5	30
Content –Concrete and well–developed ideas –No extraneous material –Essay reflects thoughts	 10 5 10	25
Grammar and vocabulary –Correct use of grammar (e.g., verb tense, prepositions, etc.) –No fragments or run–on sentences –Precise vocabulary use	 10 10 10	30

211

Mechanics -Spelling -Punctuation -Neatness	 5 5 5	15
Total Scores		100

As in Example 7.2, holistic scoring is based on an overall impression of the writing performance, and this may be considered easier to use than analytic scoring since it has less items to be evaluated. This may be true. However, at the same time, holistic scoring may be more difficult for learners who are not experienced in evaluating other's work because it requires the rater's discerning eye to see the whole picture. Regardless of the type of evaluation, raters need to be trained. If the teacher wants to include learner self-evaluation and/ or peer-evaluation in the lesson, it is very important to teach, demonstrate, and train how to do it.

• Using Collaborative Writing

Writing is commonly considered solitary work, but it can be done as a collaborative activity in the classroom. Collaborative writing has many theoretical and practical benefits. Vygostsky in his theory of *zone of proximal development* (ZPD) claims that working with others can provide the opportunity for learners to work at a level slightly above their usual capacity, as co-operating with others who know a little more can boost success. Storch (2005) also found that texts produced by pairs are better in terms of task fulfillment, grammatical accuracy

212

and complexity. This finding suggests that the process of working together provides learners with the opportunities for giving each other useful feedback, and thereby producing more accurate and complex texts. Collaborative writing has been shown to reduce anxiety and foster self-confidence, compared with completing tasks individually (Raimes, 1998; Reid & Powers, 1993; Rollinson, 2005). In addition, collaborative writing can increase motivation, risk-taking, and tolerance among learners. Discussing the writing process also provides more opportunities for learners to develop their communicative ability by forcing the negotiation of meaning. Some of the ideas of collaborative writing are below:

Example 7.4 Jigsaw Writing

Picture stories or cartoon strips are useful for this type of activity. The teacher puts students into small groups and gives each student one or two pictures from the sequence. Each student has a different picture(s). Students have to describe what is happening or happened in their picture(s). Then, the teacher asks students to share their own stories with the group members. Students in groups need to decide on the correct order of the pictures and make any changes necessary to make their paragraphs coherent.

Example 7.5 Chain Writing

Students sit in a circle and each student has a blank sheet. The teacher dictates a sentence (e.g., A boy lived in a small town). Students all write it at the top of their piece of paper. Each student is told to write the next sentence and then pass their paper to the left and each student writes the next sentence of the story they now have. The papers are then passed to the left again. This procedure continues until each student has their original paper. They are then told to write the last line(s) of the story.

• **Making Feedback Helpful and Meaningful**

Teachers provide feedback to student writing with the intention of helping students. However, teacher feedback is not always helpful (Truscott, 1996). In order to make feedback more effective, first, feedback needs be as specific as possible. In other words, the teacher needs to supply students with specific information about what they are doing is right or wrong. For instance, feedback like "Rewrite" does not give students any insights into what they did wrong and what they need to change. Instead, the teacher needs to take the time to tell students about what exactly they did well, and what may still need improvement.

Second, the teacher needs to teach students how to use correction symbols. In order to avoid an overabundance of red ink, many teachers use correction symbols and this also helps students think about what the mistake is and correct it themselves. However, in order for students to benefit from the use of symbols, they need to be trained in their use: first, the teacher needs to explain what each symbol means and demonstrate how to correct an error referring to the symbol. Then, the teacher hands the students some incorrect sentences with symbols included and has them identify the type of errors and write the sentences correctly.

Using student-teacher conferences is a good way to offer effective feedback. Conferences focus on providing individualized suggestions and comments. During the conference, the teacher needs to allow students to ask questions. It is important to set up these conferences in a structured way, so both teacher and student make good use of their time. Students are given multiple opportunities to make sure they are on the right track and make necessary improvements to their work.

• Types of Classroom Writing Activities

Teachers need to employ a variety of types of activities depending on the goal of the lesson and learners' proficiency and needs. Here are five different types of activities which can be placed at a continuum from most to least controlled activities.

1. Copying

Copying is a useful way for students to teach how to form letters and words from a given model. At the beginning stages of learning, writing letters, tracing (using tracing paper or following dotted lines) or copying lines of letters or words can be a good practice. Copying can be done in a more interesting way, using so-called 'disguised word copying' (Harmer, 2011). The teacher gives students a list of words they have recently met and asks them to write down their five most favorite and five least favorite words from the list. See another example below:

Example 7.6: Social Networking is Good and Bad for Teenagers?

Write the following sentences about social networking in the correct columns:

Social networking is an extension of teens' real-world friendships.

Social networking lessens face-to-face interaction with family and friends.

Social networking can cause online bullying by peers, also

known as cyberbullying.
Socializing online can give shy teens a comfortable way to communicate.

Social networking is good.	Social networking is bad.

Dictation also falls into this category. Dictation is the process of writing down what someone else has said. Dictation has numerous uses in the language classroom and it only requires very little preparation. It can be an effective tool for working on accuracy in writing and listening. When students do the dictating rather than teacher, speaking and pronunciation skills can improve as well. In addition, dictation activities where students compare their version of the text to the original can increase their ability to notice aspects of the language which are sometimes overlooked, as well as mistakes which they commonly make.

2. Controlled Practice

Controlled practice is often used for grammar reinforcement. Students are given models and then have to write similar sentences or paragraphs based on information they are given. This type of writing does not allow creativity on the part of the writer. In Example 7.7, students are given information about a particular character. The given model sentences show how this information can be combined in sentences with 'and' and 'but.'

Example 7.7: 'And' and 'But'

Look at the following information about Kevin's likes (√) and dislikes (X) and read the sentences which follow.

216

Kevin

Music: K–pop (√), classical music (X)
Sport: basketball (√), tennis (√)
Entertainment: films (√), clubs (√)
Food: spicy food (√), raw fish (X)

He likes K–pop but he doesn't like classical music.
He likes basketball and tennis.
He likes watching films and going out to clubs.
He likes spicy food but he doesn't like raw fish.

Now write similar sentences saying what music, sport, entertainment, and food you like. Use 'and' and 'but.'

Example 7.8: Paragraph Construction

Students read the following paragraph:

Steve Jobs co–founded Apple Computers with Steve Wozniak. He was born in San Francisco, California, on February 24, 1955. He invented iPod, iPhone, iPad, and many other innovative devices. He died in Palo Alto, California, on October, 2001.

After the teacher has made sure they have understood the information about Steve Jobs, students are given the following table of information and asked to write a similar paragraph about Henry Ford:

Name	Henry Ford
Occupation	Founder of Ford Motor Company
Date of birth	July 30, 1863
Place of birth	Greenfield Township, Michigan
Examples of work	Ford Quadricycle, Ford Model T, etc.
Died	April 7, 1947

Example 7.8 employs a substitution–drill type of exercise in that new vocabulary is used within a set pattern or patterns. Students are required to write a paragraph which is almost identical to one they have read using the given information.

3. Guided Writing

It is a type of controlled practice, but considered as slightly less controlled. One way of doing guided writing involves the teacher using a series of questions. For instance, after reading a text or watching a videotape, the teacher asks the students to write about what they read and watched using questions like "Where does the story take place?" and "What does the man do for his girlfriend?"

Another form of controlled writing is dicto–comp (also called dictogloss). In dicto–comp, students recreate a text or story that the teacher reads to them: In order to employ dicto–comp effectively, it is important to choose a text that suits the level of the learners (e.g., beginners – 3 to 4 sentences; intermediate – 6 to 8 sentences; advanced – 8 to 12 sentences). It has four stages:

(1) Preparation: The teacher introduces the topic, if necessary, the language focus and the key vocabulary.

(2) Dictation: The teacher reads the text at a slightly slower speed than native speaker speed. Read the text again at native speaker speed and, on the second reading, students individually make very brief notes (sentence fragments) on main ideas. Remember that the purpose is to get the main ideas, not every word exactly as it appears in the text, so do not read too slowly.

(3) Reconstruction: Students reconstruct the passage in pairs by comparing notes and write a shared version of the text, editing for accurate punctuation, spelling and inclusion of the main ideas.

(4) Analysis and correction – Students compare reconstructions with other groups and with the original. Discuss the differences.

218

Dicto-comp activities have several advantages. They integrate the four language skills of listening, reading, speaking, and writing. They also give students opportunities to talk both about content and about the language itself. Furthermore, they give support to less confident students, as they are encouraged to participate in their groups as part of the structure of the activity.

4. Self-writing

Self-writing includes writing with only the self in mind as an audience. Note-taking students do during a lecture falls into self-writing. Journal writing may be the most commonly known self-writing. In some cases, dialogue journal can be used as a tool of self-writing practice and communication between the teacher and the student: a student writes thoughts and feelings, and a teacher reads and responds to it.

5. Real Writing

In the classroom, writing is very often used to practice language and display knowledge (e.g., examination). However, in reality, people write for many different purposes. Brown (2007) categorizes the types of real writing into three groups: academic writing, vocational/technical writing, and personal writing. Academic writing includes any types of writing people do to develop and share their knowledge in certain fields and logical thoughts. Vocational/technical writing includes writing people do in their occupation (e.g., business letters and directions for some operation). Personal writing includes letters, postcards, personal messages, and other informal writing. It can be done for communication with others or only for the writer.

219

Chapter Concluding Remarks

When we write, many different skills and knowledge, such as spelling, grammar, vocabulary, context, content, etc., are required. In other words, writing is not just about using language, but it is more about organizing thoughts logically, accurately, and properly. This explains why it takes time and effort to develop writing skills in both first and second languages. In addition, not many people would say that they enjoy writing. Fortunately, writing is a teachable and learnable skill, and the teacher can play an invaluable role in helping learners develop and enjoy writing. To do so, first and foremost, it is important for the teacher to identify learners' needs and interests (e.g., purpose of learning, levels, favorable topics, etc.), and this understanding enables her to create effective and enjoyable writing instruction. It is also crucial to help learners to understand the process of writing by guiding them through the steps of creating ideas, drafting, feedback, and revision since learners will be able to realize that writing is a good way of developing logical thinking skills and language skills as well.

220

Chapter

8

Teaching Grammar

Chapter 8.

Teaching Grammar

Grammar is generally defined as the set of rules that explains how words are used in a language. The role of grammar in second language classrooms has been valued differently depending on the teaching method and era. In the grammar translation method and cognitive approach, teaching language forms was considered essential in second language class. However, with the influence of Krashen's (1982) argument that grammar can be acquired naturally through meaningful input and opportunities to interact in the classroom, anti-grammar movement was dominant in the 1980s. In other words, proponents of Krashen believed that grammar competence can develop in a fluency-oriented environment without conscious attention to language forms. However, this so-called 'zero option approach' started losing support when research showed evidence revealing that the fluency-oriented environment is limited in developing accuracy in learners' language (Ellis, 1993). This resulted in a resurgence of interest in the role of grammar instruction in second language learning. Recent views of second language methodology mostly accept the importance of some form-focused instruction within the communicative frame work. This does not mean that we need to go back to the era of the grammar translation method. In fact, we should not. Learners need to study grammar in order to correctly use the language not to build up knowledge about the language. This chapter will introduce different approaches to grammar instruction teachers should know in order to design effective grammar lessons and activities that can be used in the classroom.

Principles for Teaching Grammar

• Deductive vs. Inductive Approaches

Grammar instruction can be classified into deductive approach and inductive approach. In the deductive classroom, the teacher provides a grammatical explanation or rule followed by a set of exercises. In the inductive classroom, the teacher gives learners samples of language and guides students to discover a rule for themselves. In other words, deductive approach is essentially a top-down approach which moves from the more general to the more specific. Inductive approach is more of a bottom-up approach, moving from the more specific to the more general (see Example 8.1 and Example 8.2).

Example 8.1: Deductive Grammar Teaching

Compare adjective ending in –**ing** and –**ed**:

The –**ing** adjective tells you about the job.

My work is boring/interesting/tiring/satisfying/depressing.

The –**ed** adjective tells you how somebody feels about the job.

I'm bored with my work.

I'm not interested in my work anymore.

I'm always tired when I get home after work.

I'm not satisfied with my work. My work makes me depressed.

1. Complete the sentences below for each situation. Use the word in parentheses + –**ing** or –**ed**.

(1) The opera wasn't as interesting as we had expected. (disappoint)

(a) The opera was ____________

(b) We were _____________ in the opera.

(2) Jennifer works in kindergarten. It's a very hard job, but she loves her job. (exhaust)

(a) She enjoys her job, but it's often _______.

(b) At the end of a day's work, she is often ________.

Example 8.2: Inductive Grammar Teaching

These pairs of adjectives ending in –**ed** and –**ing** describe how something feels or how something makes someone feel.

surprised/surprising	interested/interesting
bored/boring	excited/exciting
tired/tiring	confused/confusing
disappointed/disappointing	frighten/frightening

1. Look at the underlined words in the sentences below.

(a) Charles is interested in sport. He thinks baseball is the most interesting.

(b) Adams looked frightened as the movie he was watching became more and more frightening.

(c) We all felt disappointed about the terrible and disappointing news.

(d) Some of my classes are very boring. I get most bored in math lessons.

(e) I felt very annoyed. The most annoying thing was his way of talking.

First, write down those which the **–ing** words refer to.

(a) (b) (c) (d) (e)

Then write down those which the **–ed** words refer to.

(a) (b) (c) (d) (e)

Both Example 8.1 and Example 8.2 target the same language form- adjective ending in '–ing' and '–ed,' but they differ in how to teach it. Example 8.1 first offers the rule followed by some example sentences while Example 8.2 provides examples with the target form first, and then, learners are required to generate the rule based on the given examples.

Both deductive and inductive teaching have their pros and cons. The deductive approach gets straight to the point, and can therefore be time-saving. Adult learners, especially, learners who have an analytical learning style, tend to prefer this type of instruction. In contrast, children and young learners may have difficulty in understanding the concepts involved. In addition, rule explanation is often delivered using metalanguage (i.e., language used to talk about language such as grammar terminology), so it may not be beneficial

226

for learners who are not familiar with the grammar terms. Deductive instruction is usually teacher-fronted and learners are recipients of information the teacher delivers.

In inductive learning environment, in contrast, learners are more actively engaged in the learning process rather than being passive recipients. This increased engagement may help learners to develop a deeper understanding of the language being learned. In addition, this can promote the strategy of 'noticing' in the student and enhance learner autonomy and motivation. On the other hand, inductive learning can be more time and energy consuming and more demanding of the teacher and the learner. It is also possible that learners may arrive at an incorrect inference or produce an incorrect or incomplete rule. Also, an inductive approach may frustrate learners whose personal learning style is more in line with being taught by a teacher-centered and deductive approach.

As noted above, there are pros and cons to both approaches, and a combination of both inductive and deductive grammar teaching and learning is probably inevitable since learners will get various benefits from the both approaches depending on their age, levels, and cognitive styles and characteristics of language forms.

• Form-Meaning-Function Mapping

Larsen-Freeman (2001) claims that grammar should not be considered as a discrete set of meaningless and decontextualized structures to teach grammar within a communicative framework. She emphasizes that grammatical structures "not only have (morphosyntactic) form, they are also used to express meaning (semantics) in context appropriate use (pragmatics)" (p. 252). Form refers to the mechanics of the language (i.e., morphosyntactic, lexical patterns, and phonemic/graphemic patterns). In other words, it is concerned with how a particular grammar structure is constructed and how it is sequenced with other structures in a sentence or text. Meaning refers to both lexical (a dictionary definition) and grammatical meanings. Use refers to how grammar is used in a social context (a context created by the relationship between interlocutors and settings) and linguistic discourse context (language used in a particular genre or register of discourse or the language that precedes or follows a particular structure in the discourse).

The following examples show what form, meaning, and function mean in a particular grammar point.

Example 8.3: Past Perfect Tense

Form: Subject + had + past participle + object/complement

Meaning: Earlier actions/events in a narrative

Function: The past perfect tense is usually used in conjunction with the past tense. The past perfect is used to order events, so subsequent sentences usually appear in the simple past (e.g., Tom had studied English for ten years. As a result, he got a great job in England last year).

Example 8.4: Possessive

Form: Adding an apostrophe + s ('s) for a singular noun, adding an apostrophe after the 's' ending (s'). Three allomorphs /z/, /s/, and /əz/ occurs after sibilants.

Meaning: It shows that something belongs to someone or

228

something (e.g., Jane's computer) and indicates time and duration (e.g., one week's holiday).
Function: 's is used as a determiner (possessive determiner), the periphrastic of the form (e.g., the legs of the table), and noun compounds (table leg).

Understanding three dimensions is essential for learners to use grammatical structures accurately, meaningfully, and appropriately. Larsen-Freeman (1997, 2001) points out that grammar teaching is not about knowledge transmission but about skill development, using the term 'grammaring' – grammar is "a skill to be mastered, rather than a set of rules to be memorized" (Larsen-Freeman, 2001, p. 255).

Helping learners understand form-meaning-function of a grammar structure does not necessarily mean that the class time needs to be devoted to grammar explanation. Indeed, if the teacher wants to effectively cover form, meaning, and use in the classroom, he needs to keep the explanation brief. Instead, a visual diagram and several examples also further highlight the target form. In addition, the teacher needs to devote several lessons to a specific grammar or language point. This allows the teacher to address and practice the rules and exceptions, without overwhelming the class with too much information. The teacher should also provide several opportunities to acquire the target language during a course of study. By revisiting the target structures, students who grasped the form have a second chance to understand the meaning and use of the target structure. Students who grasped the meaning have a second chance for the form and use.

229

Classroom Instruction

• Presentation-Practice-Production vs. Task-Based Grammar Instruction

Presentation-practice-production (PPP)

PPP is one of most commonly used approaches to teach grammar in second language classrooms. A PPP lesson, as its name suggests, is divided into three phases. First, the teacher presents the target language, and then students practice the new language items. Finally, they produce their own ideas to talk about themselves. The assumption behind this approach is that knowledge becomes skills through successive practice and accuracy precedes fluency.

The presentation phase is controlled by the teacher. For instance, if the aim of the lesson is to teach the 'present continuous for arrangements,' the teacher asks the students about some activities they plan to do this coming weekend. Then, suggested ideas are written on the board using the present continuous. This way, the 'present continuous' is being presented in a contextualized way. Alternatively, the teacher might present the 'present continuous' without reference to a situation through description supplemented with examples.

In the practice stage, the teacher provides the students with the opportunities to practice the learned item in a controlled way such as drills, multiple-choice exercises, gap-filling exercises, and transformations. In this phase, the teacher's role is to direct the activities, provide positive feedback to students, correct mistakes, and model the correct forms. The focus is on form.

Once the students have completely mastered the form, it is time for them to use the newly learned language structure to produce oral or written texts. Typical production activities include dialogues, oral presentations, and the production of sentences, paragraphs or longer texts. The production stage focuses on fluency and provides students with an opportunity to personalize the language learned by doing less controlled tasks and free tasks (e.g., role-play). The teacher does not generally intervene or correct in this phase. If errors are made, they are pointed out after the exercise has finished. As a rough ideal proportion of time spent on each of three stages of PPP in a lesson should be something like 1:2:3.

It is easy to prepare and practice a PPP lesson in the classroom. However, this does not necessarily mean that it is an effective way to learn grammar. It is often observed that the PPP approach uses simplistic, mechanical imitation, and repetition in the practice stage, but this is far from the way to establish form-meaning connections. The PPP approach is similar with skill-based language teaching in that it also involves employing activities or practice after declarative explanation of target items (Dekeyser, 1998). However, parrot-like repetitive practice does not help students make form-meaning mapping (Yamaoka, 2005). Instead, a large amount of practice in context is required so that *declarative knowledge* can develop into *procedural knowledge*. It is desirable to provide practice which allows learners to use the target rules or expressions repeatedly in a context where a connection between form and meaning can be established (DeKeyser, 2001).

231

Task-based grammar instruction

Task-based grammar instruction focuses on a language task rather than a grammar rule. The language is used to complete a task. The syllabus for task-based grammar instruction is not designed by a list of specific grammar points; rather, it is based on different types of language tasks (e.g., negotiation, problem solving, interviewing, etc.) that students should be able to accomplish. Thus, students are capable of using the language in the context which is similar with real-life situations. Naturally, when the teacher plans a lesson based on task-based instruction, her goal is to create situations where students must use a given language structure to accomplish their tasks. But, the first priority is the language task and not the grammar.

Task-based grammar instruction can be practiced in various versions. Here are three stages to plan a lesson: pre-task, task cycle, and language focus stage. In the pre-task stage, teachers should choose the goal of a lesson, then, identify the necessary language skills to accomplish the goal. For example, if the goal of the lesson is negotiating a contract in business, students will need to know specific business vocabulary, and they will also need to negotiate using polite suggestions (e.g., What if my company did A for you and your company did B for us?) and other necessary expressions and structures. After the teacher decides the goal of a lesson and identifies necessary and appropriate language skills required to accomplish the goal are identified, she introduces the lesson to the students by telling them the goal of the given task and reviewing any grammatical structures and vocabulary that will be necessary to accomplish the task. However, the teacher should not have students practice the different grammar points in isolation from the main goal of the lesson.

Subsequently, students perform the task by interacting with one another within the set parameters to accomplish their language goal. Tasks might include playing a game, sharing an experience, or participating in a role play that requires problem-solving. While they do the assigned language task, they may use the grammar structures the teacher has presented, but they do not have to. The goal of the task is to achieve the goal, and, as long as students accomplish it, the task is successful. At this point, students might also make errors with the grammatical concepts introduced by the teacher, but the teacher should not explicitly correct them. Instead, the teacher needs to encourage students to use language fluently even if it comes at the cost of accuracy. After students finish the task, they are given some time to reflect on how they accomplished it. The teacher can have them discuss the activity in the groups they performed or write out how they accomplished the language goal such as whether they used the grammatical structures the teacher presented or not, and what other strategies they used. Then, the groups share with the rest of the class how they accomplished their goals either orally or in writing.

In the language focus stage, the teacher draws students' attention to specific language structures. In this stage, students practice a particular structure and the teacher provides feedback on accuracy. This looks more like traditional grammar classes, but it comes at the end of the lesson and is not emphasized at the cost of fluency. After that, if necessary, students are asked to perform the task again.

233

As opposed to the PPP model, task-based grammar instruction adopts a fluency-to-accuracy sequence. In other words, learners start by expressing themselves using their available resources, and they then receive guidance (e.g., error correction and explicit instruction) as to how to improve their performance. Through successive stages of trial, error, and feedback, learner output is fine-tuned for accuracy.

Characteristics of PPP vs. Task-based grammar instruction

PPP and task-based learning (TBL) are different in many aspects as shown in Table 8.1.

TABLE 8.1

Different Features of PPP and TBL

	PPP	TBL
Teacher's role	Presenting a language form and conducing practice	Selecting tasks and sequencing them
Primary focus	Form (moving from accuracy to fluency)	Meaning (moving from fluency from accuracy)
Skills	Discrete form	Integrated skills
Real-life relation	Not related: Discouraging students from experimenting and working things out for themselves	Closely related: Encouraging coping strategies and creativity
Language exposure	Limited	Rich and Varied

Which is more effective than the other? PPP has been criticized for its effectiveness in second language learning, while many second language research findings and educators advocate task-based grammar instruction. This may lead us to the conclusion that students benefit more from task-based instruction than PPP. This can be true, but task-based instruction does not fit all classes; for instance, if the class size is too big and if students prefer a straightforward lesson, PPP may be more appropriate than task-based instruction. Although the traditional PPP approach has its inherent problem – it does not result in proper form-meaning mapping, if a PPP lesson is conducted with more contextualized practices, this shortcoming could be minimized. Teachers should be flexible in choosing which approach needs to be employed to provide the most effective lesson for their learners.

• Input-Based Grammar Instruction

Most of the traditional grammar instructions and exercises are output-oriented. In other words, students are asked to use the target form from the beginning. Unlike this traditional approach, input-based instruction focuses on boosting the way in which input is internalized or processed (i.e., input becomes intake). Ellis (2012) defines input-based instruction as an instruction that "involves the manipulation of the input that learners are exposed to or are required to process" (p. 285). In other words, learners are exposed to input which is carefully designed to facilitate learners' internalization of input. This section introduces two major input-based instructional strategies which can be easily conducted in the classroom: input enhancement and processing instruction.

235

Input enhancement

Input enhancement is defined as "the process by which language input becomes salient to learners" (Sharwood Smith, 1991, p. 118). In other words, input enhancement can be used to draw learners' attention to the target forms by using special techniques such as, bolding, *italicizing*, and CAPITALIZING. For example, if the target feature is a passive verb, the teacher provides learners with a reading passage where passive verb forms are highlighted, and they then are asked to read the passage and answer the comprehension questions or comprehension-based activities. In other words, students' attention is drawn to the passive form, but the primary focus of the lesson is on meaning, understanding the passage. See an example of input enhancement below:

> **Example 8.5: Input Enhancement**
>
> Instruction: Please read the text and then answer the following questions.
>
> A girl decided to go **cycling** for the day. She called her friends and asked them if they would be interested in **joining** her. They thought that **biking** would be an **exciting** thing to do on such a hot day. The girl and her friends took their bikes up a steep road, and went **flying** down the big hill. Many hours later, they finished **having** their fun and went home again.
>
> **Questions**
>
> 1. Why did the girl call her friends?
> 2. Where did they go biking?
> 3. Did they enjoy biking?
>
> (Adapted from Nassaji & Fotos, 2011, pp. 45–46)

236

A great deal of second language research has been conducted to examine the effectiveness of input enhancement. They reached the following conclusions: (a) simple enhancement is capable of inducing learner noticing of externally enhanced forms in meaning-bearing input; (b) whether or not it leads to acquisition depends largely on whether the learner has prior knowledge of the target form; (c) learners may automatically notice forms that are meaningful; (d) simple enhancement is more effective if it draws focal rather than peripheral attention (Nassaji & Fotos, 2011). In order to effectively practice input enhancement in the classroom, the teacher especially needs to attend to the first two findings. It is possible to draw learner attention to enhanced forms while learners process input for meaning; however, learners' prior knowledge largely affects the extent to which such noticing leads to acquisition.

Processing instruction

One form of input-based instruction is Processing Instruction (PI) (e.g., Lee & VanPatten, 2003; VanPatten, 1993, 1996) based on VanPatten's model of input processing. He accepts the importance of input, but he claims that simple exposure to input is not sufficient to bring about acquisition since learners tend to pay attention to meaning not form. Input processing for meaning does not always result in acquiring grammar (Sharwood Smith, 1991, 1993). As a solution to this problem, he argues that learners need to be taught how to process input in order to better acquire the underlying grammar. PI entails pushing learners to recognize the grammar in the input.

There are three basic components to PI:

1. Learners are provided with explanations of the grammar.

2. Learners are alerted to problems they may encounter with the input, particularly those caused by differences between the grammar of the target language and the native language.

3. Learners engaged in structured input activities: referential and affective activities.

In referential activities, there is always a right or wrong answer. For instance, learners are asked to choose between two nouns that are associated with a given picture. Their answers reveal whether they have correctly understood the meaning. In contrast, affective activities are activities which do not have any right or wrong answer. Learners are required to provide an affective response by indicating their opinions about events. Structured input activities can be conducted in both oral and written form. See an example of PI below:

Example 8.6: Processing Instruction

Target form: third–person singular '–s' verb form

Learners of English often drop the '–s' when the verb is in the third person singular form because the meaning of third person singular is already mentioned by the subject (e.g., he, she, and it). The following activities will help learners attend to verb forms in order to get meaning.

▷ **Referential activity**

David is a college freshmen. In a discussion about the benefits and risks of on–line dating, David expresses views that are typically very different from his group members. Read the sentences below and indicate (√) whether each view expressed belongs to David or to David's classmates, and then indicate whether David is more positive or negative about on–line dating compared to his group members.

David	His group members	Opinions
		think that online dating provides individuals with access to many more potential partners than they could often find in their daily lives.
		trust that many online dating sites offer various types of personality testing and matching.
		believes the choices of partners can become confusing and overwhelming.
		claims that matching is a difficult process and testing may not be accurate for everyone.
		believe that online dating offers a number of ways to get to know a potential date before meeting in person.
		thinks that communication through computers is lacking some of the information provided in face-to-face interaction.

Choose one:

David has positive opinions about on-line dating. _________

David has negative opinions about on-line dating. _________

▷ **Affective activity**

Read the following sentences. Are they true for a typical student at your school?

The typical student …	True	False
1. gets up at 7:00 a.m.	_____	_____
2. skips breakfast.	_____	_____
3. makes his bed every day.	_____	_____
4. works part time.	_____	_____
5. skips at least one class a week.	_____	_____
6. cooks dinner every evening.	_____	_____
7. has a boy or girl friend.	_____	_____

239

Input enhancement and processing instruction are both based on Schmidt's noticing hypothesis (1990, 2001): "people learn about the things that they attend to and do not learn much about the things they do not attend to" (Schmidt, 2001, p. 30). By textually enhancing or structuring language forms, it is expected that students will pay their attention to the forms. Although they have in common that both are input-based and put an emphasis on the role of noticing, they differ in the way of drawing student attention to form. In input enhancement, the teacher does not mention about which forms students need to focus on while they read a given text. In contrast, processing instruction explicitly points out which grammar form will be covered and problems students have with the form. In short, they differ in terms of the degree of explicitness.

• Classroom Techniques and Activities

Grammar activities and techniques can be classified in a different way. This section will use a typical classification which has been widely used in the field of second language instruction (i.e., controlled vs. free techniques) (Ur, 2012).

In conventional grammar instruction, the teacher helps students make the leap from form-focused grammar exercise to fluent production exercise. Below is a description of grammar activities that deal with different grammar features moving from very controlled and accuracy-based activities to fluency activities.

Example 8.7 Controlled Drills

Students produce examples of the structure which are predetermined by the teacher or materials. Students can do this type of activity without understanding meaning.

Target form: Present simple

Write or say about Patrick, using the following examples.

Patrick drinks tea but he doesn't drink coffee.

a) Like: pastas/pizza   b) speak: Spanish/ Italian

b) play: football/ basketball   d) take: a math class/a history class

Example 8.8 Controlled Responses through Sentences Completion

Students are given a direction to reproduce examples of the structure. Their understanding of meaning is required.

Target form: Passive

Rewrite the sentence so that it means the same, but using the given word.

I received a direction. (give)

He received $500. (pay)

Example 8.9 Meaningful Drills

Students' responses are very controlled, but they can make limited choices and needs to understand the meaning to answer correctly.

Target form: Present simple tense

Choose your close friends, and write down their names. Now compose true statements about them according to the following model:

He/She likes ice cream; or He/She doesn't like ice cream.

enjoy: play tennis   b) drink: wine   c) speak: French

241

Example 8.10 Guided, Meaningful Practice

Students make a sentence using a given structure, but they have a choice in vocabulary.

Target form: Conditional clauses

Use the following cue: If I had a million dollars,

Complete the sentence saying or writing what you would do.

Example 8. 11 Structure-Based Free Sentence Composition

Students are given a visual cue (e.g., a picture) and asked to describe the picture orally and in written form.

Target form: Present progressive

Look at the picture and describe what is going on.

Example 8.12 Structure-Based Discourse Composition

Students talk about and write about the given issue, using at least some examples of the structure within the discourse.

Target form: Modal

Recommend solutions to the following case: You see a good friend of yours cheating in an exam. What might you do? Your recommendations should include the modals (might, should, must, can, could, etc.).

It is important to remember that the controlled-free scale does not correspond to the beginning-through-advanced proficiency continuum. There are cases where even advanced learners need controlled activities (e.g., having a problem with a particular language form). Likewise, the teacher needs to employ free activities to help beginning learners develop fluency.

242

Chapter Concluding Remarks

Nowadays, developing communicative ability in second language is regarded as essential in language education. Thus, meaning-based classroom instruction has been conceived as an ideal condition for language learning. This may be true. However, the field of second language acquisition has witnessed that learners in pure meaning/communication-based classes where teaching language forms is ignored do not successfully develop their second language. If we consider a growing body of research evidence that supports the role of grammar instruction in second language development, it is not necessary to argue whether or not grammar teaching is important any more. What is more important is how to include grammar instruction in communicative language classrooms. Various approaches and activities for grammar instruction addressed in this chapter may be useful for teachers to design grammar lessons which can eventually help learners' development of communicative ability.

243

Chapter

9

Planning a Lesson

Chapter 9.

Planning a Lesson

A lesson plan is the teacher's plan for what to teach, how to teach, and how to check students' understanding. A successful lesson plan addresses and integrates three key components: objectives for students learning, teaching and learning activities, and strategies to check student understanding. Richards (1998) notes that lesson plans help the teacher consider the lesson in advance to "resolve problems and difficulties, to provide a structure for a lesson, to provide a 'map' for the teacher to follow, and to provide a record of what has been taught" (p. 103). In addition, teachers gain confidence about the lesson since they can learn the subject matter better and anticipate problems before they happen while planning a lesson. In this chapter, crucial elements in planning a lesson will be discussed, focusing on three phrases: design, implementation, and reflection.

247

Designing a Plan

• Lesson Objectives

An effective lesson plan starts by specifying concrete objectives for student learning. An objective is a description of a learning outcome. A well-written objective statement provides a clear picture of the outcome or performance as a result of the lesson. It should be specific, concise, and, most importantly, observable or measurable. The ABCD method of writing objectives is an excellent way to structure instructional objectives. In this method, A is for audience, B is for behavior, C is for conditions, and D is for degree of mastery needed (see TABLE 9.1).

TABLE 9.1

ABCD Method of Writing Objectives

Objective Part	Description	Example
Audience (A)	Who will do	Students
Behavior (B)	What they will be able to do	Will be able to re-write the sentence in future tense
Condition (C)	How they will able to do it	Given a sentence written in the past or present tense
Degree of mastery (D)	Degree of accuracy observed	With no errors in terms of tense

More examples are presented below:

- Given four works of short fiction of diverse genres, the student will be able to analyze and match each work with its correct genre.
- Using the koreaherald.com web site, the student will correctly identify and print out two examples each of a news article and an editorial on an issue related to English education.
- Given ten examples of incorrect verb tense usage, the student will identify and correct a minimum of eight instances.

When writing the objective of lesson, the greatest challenge for a pre-service/novice teacher is choosing the right verb. A lesson objective should describe the measurable and observable aspects of students' performance. Thus, verbs such as 'understand, know, perceive, and learn' should not be used. Instead, action verbs such as 'select, identify, match, and analyze' are proper. Bloom's Taxonomy and associate action verbs provide some tips for choosing right verbs for writing a lesson objective (see TABLE 9.2).

TABLE 9.2

Writing Objectives for Lesson Plans Using Bloom's Taxonomy and Associated Action or Performance Verbs

Learning level	Associated action verbs
Knowledge	define, describe, state, list, name, write, recall, recognize, label, underline, select, reproduce, outline, match
Comprehension	identify, justify, select, indicate, illustrate, represent, name, formulate, explain, judge, contrast, classify
Application	predict, select, assess, explain, choose, find, show, demonstrate, construct, compute, use, perform
Analysis	analyze, identify, conclude, differentiate, select, separate, compare, contrast, justify, resolve, break down, criticize

249

Synthesis	combine, restate, summarize, precise, argue, discuss, organize, derive, select, relate, generalize, conclude
Evaluation	judge, evaluate, determine, recognize, support, defend, attack, criticize, identify, avoid, select, choose

The verbs listed above provide a guide on what to observe since they describe actions. One of the crucial reasons why lesson objectives should be specific and observable is because whether or not learners achieve the objectives is a critical point of assessing their performance in the lesson. In other words, the objectives provide the teacher with the elements that will be evaluated.

• Activities and Procedures

After writing the lesson objectives, teachers need to decide which activities and procedures they will use to ensure the successful achievement of the objectives. Teachers should think through the purposes and structures of the activities and remember that activities which are relevant to students' real-life and situations increase their interest in the lesson and their intrinsic motivation as well. As teachers plan the examples and activities, it is essential to estimate how much time is needed for each one. It is also useful to prepare an extra activity in case class time is left.

Two issues should be considered when teachers choose activities - variety and pacing (Richards, 2008). To vary activities, teacher should think through the characteristics of activities. The following elements need to be considered:

specific language and other skills required to complete an activity, the flexibility of the outcome, the necessity of meaning negotiation, the class organization (e.g., individual task, pair work, group work, or whole class interaction), and the level of difficulty. Variety in a lesson is important for many reasons. For example, it might be a way to satisfy students with different characteristics (e.g., personality, aptitude, etc.). More specifically, if students who are intrapersonal and introverted keep being asked to work in groups, it might be burdensome for them. If students who are kinesthetic are asked to understand a concept through reading, it might not be effective. In addition, employing various activities can make the class more interesting and dynamic. Using proper and interesting activities for students will eventually trigger their intrinsic motivation. Another issue is pacing and it is linked to the length of an activity, relevance among activities, and a smooth movement from one activity to the other. In other words, activities should not be too long or too short, they should well flow together, and there should be clear transitions between each activity (Brown, 2007).

• Consolidation

As a means of concluding the lesson, the materials covered in class need to be reviewed by summarizing the main points of the lesson. Teachers can do this in a number of ways: they can state the main points themselves ("Today we talked about…"), they can ask a student to summarize the points, or they can even ask all students to write down the main points of the lesson on a piece of paper. Teachers can review the students' answers to gauge their understanding of the topic and then explain anything unclear in the following class. Teachers also conclude the lesson not only by summarizing the main points, but also by previewing the next lesson and pointing out how the day's topic relates to the following lesson. This preview can spur students' interest and help them connect the different ideas within a larger context.

Implementing the Plan

Implementing the lesson plan is the most important and difficult stage of the lesson planning cycle. As many experienced teachers know, the class sometimes does not proceed as it has been planned, and it is easy to get sidetracked by unexpected events. Teachers should remember that the plan has been made based on specific goals and diagnosis of students' competence, needs, and interests. Thus, it is important to follow the original plan. However, teachers also need to make immediate adjustments to the original plan when it is necessary. Richards (2008) suggests two cases where teachers might need to deviate from the original one. First, "when the lesson is obviously going badly and the plan is not helping to produce the desired outcome; second, when something happens during an early part of the lesson that necessitates improvisation" (p. 43). For novice teachers, it is difficult to develop contingency plans to substitute the original

252

plan, but they must deal with unexpected situations quickly, and this kind of professional knowledge will be developed with experience.

Reflecting on the Lesson

A lesson plan may not work as well as teachers have expected due to a number of extraneous circumstances, but there is no reason to be discouraged. It happens to even to the most experienced teachers. What is important for teachers is to reflect on what worked well and badly, why, and what they could have done differently. Identifying successful and less successful organization of class time and activities would make it easier to adjust to the contingencies of the classroom.

Chapter Concluding Remarks

The lesson plan does not have to be an exhaustive document that describes each and every possible classroom scenario. Instead, it should provide the teacher with a general outline of teaching goals, learning objectives, and means to accomplish them. A lesson plan is like a road map which describes where the teacher hopes to go in a lesson, presumably taking the students along (Bailey, 1996). In Bailey definition, the word 'presumably' is noticeable. More specifically, it is a plan. What would actually happen in class can be different: "In realizing lesson plans, part of a skilled teacher's logic in use involves managing such departures [from the original lesson plan] to maximize teaching and learning opportunities" (p. 38). Teachers, needless to say, should design a thoughtful lesson plan, but, at the same, they need to be equipped with flexibility in the implementation of the plan.

Chapter

10

Assessment and Testing

Chapter 10.

Assessment and Testing

The term 'assessment' may not be familiar to everyone. A test will be a more frequently used term, and it is a type of assessment. Assessment is an umbrella term for a test. Although there are many different ways to use assessment, it is mainly employed to evaluate students' overall level, progress, achievement during a course, and strengths and weaknesses. This chapter deals with different types of assessment and some of the important components of a test.

Types of Assessment

Assessment is classified according to its formality, main functions, purposes, and the method of result interpretation. This section explains eight different ways of assessing student

257

performance.

• Informal and Formal Assessment

Informal assessment allows teachers to follow the ongoing progress of their students based on observing students' performance. Teachers can recognize students' specific problem areas and adjust their instruction methods. Informal assessment can take a number of forms including all of the activities students do in the classroom and students' portfolios. Informal assessment is almost always nonjudgmental in that a teacher acts as a coach or facilitator not a judge.

Formal assessment uses formal tests or structured continuous assessment to evaluate a learner's level of language. In other words, they are preplanned and contain the formal grading system which includes interpreting results in official ways. Formal assessment takes a various form from a class quiz and a final exam in the class to standardized tests such as Test of English as a Foreign Language (TOEFL) and Test of English for International Communication (TOEIC). A test is formal assessment, but it does not mean that all formal assessment is testing. The teacher can include students' journals or portfolios as a component of formal assessment.

Informal and formal assessments both are valuable for making valid and useful assessments of students' knowledge and performance. Many teachers employ both, for example by evaluating one skill using informal assessment such as observing group work, and another using formal tools, for example a grammar test.

• Formative and Summative Assessment

Based on the different functions of assessment, it can be divided into summative assessment and formative assessment. Formative assessment is conducted in order for the teacher to use information gained from assessments about a student's progress as the basis for further classroom work. Most of the assessment the teacher carries out during a course is formative in nature. It can provide a grade in the form of a number, feedback in the form of error correction, and other suggestions for improvement. It is mainly concerned with keeping track of students' progress and the process of learning.

In contrast, summative assessment aims to measure students' achievement. It is not necessarily related immediately to what has been taught, and it is not necessarily prepared and carried out by the class teacher. It is normally carried out either by the class teacher or by an external authority such as a ministry of education and internationally recognized body (e.g., Educational Testing Service and the British Council). Korean Scholastic Assessment Test (KSAT), TOEFL, TOEIC, and International English Language Testing System (IELTS) are summative in nature. It is primarily concerned with classifying overall levels of achievement and the result of learning.

• Discrete-Point Tests and Integrative Tests

Discrete-point tests are constructed based on the assumption that language can be broken down into its component parts (i.e., skills and various units of language of phonology, morphology, lexicon, syntax, and discourse) and that those parts can be tested separately. A discrete-point test consists of many questions on a large number of linguistic points, but each question tests only one linguistic point. For example, the following multiple choice item tests only the learner's knowledge of the correct past form of the verb 'play':

Example 10.1: Discrete-point Test

When I was a kid I .... the violin.

a. play b. played c. has played d. was playing

Discrete-point tests are practical and easy to administer and grade. However, they show only students' ability to recognize or produce individual items. They do not measure how students would use the language in actual communication.

In contrast, integrative tests are constructed based on the assumption that language competence is a unified set of interacting abilities which cannot be separated apart and tested adequately (Oller, 1979). They test more than one skill and/or item of knowledge at a time. While discrete-point tests attempt to test knowledge of language one bit at a time, integrative tests attempt to assess a learner's capacity to use many bits all at the same time. Oral interviews and written compositions are typical examples of integrative tests. In the interview, for instance, test-takers have to listen to and understand the examiner's questions, choose the relevant grammar and lexis to express their ideas, speak with intelligible/accurate pronunciation and intonation. In short, test-takers are required to integrate a variety of skills and items of linguistic knowledge to complete the test.

260

Integrative tests require learners to use language similarly to the way they use it in the real world. However, it has some issues related to reliability (see the section of Principles of Assessment in this chapter). Let us assume that a student takes a composition test. Depending on how much he knows about a given topic, he might have more or less to write about the topic. In addition, there might be cases where there is a big gap between two raters' scores (e.g., one rater gave 8 out of 10, but another gave 4). In order to resolve this possible problem, rater training and use of specific scoring rubrics are essential for conversation and composition tests.

The following tests show a distinctive difference between integrative and discrete-item tests:

Example 10.2: Cloze Test (fixed-ratio deletion; every seventh word)

The recognition that one's feelings of (1)_____ and unhappiness can coexist much like (2)___ and hate in a close relationship (3)_____ offer valuable clues on how to (4)_____ a happier life. It suggests, for (5) _______ that changing or avoiding things that (6) _____ you miserable may well make you (7) _____ miserable but probably no happier.

Example 10.3: Rational Deletion (prepositions and conjunctions)

The recognition that one's feelings (1)____ happiness (2)____ unhappiness can coexist much like love and hate (3) ____ a close relationship may offer valuable clues (4) _____ how to lead a happier life. It suggests, (5) _____ example, that changing (6) ____ avoiding things that make you miserable may well make you less miserable (7) _____ probably no happier.

(Adapted from Brown & Abeywickrama, 2010, pp. 242–243)

In both examples, there are seven deletions, but the aims of these tests completely differ. There is no specific linguistic feature to be tested in Example 10.2, while prepositions and conjunctions are target features in Example 10.3. Put differently, Example 10.2 evaluates test-takers' overall ability (i.e., integrative test); Example 10.3 checks test-takers' ability in using prepositions and conjunctions (i.e., discrete-point test).

• Norm-Referenced and Criterion-Referenced Tests

Norm-referenced tests compare an examinee's performance to that of other examinees. In other words, test-takers' scores are interpreted in relation to a mean, median, and standard deviation, and percentile rank. Scores are usually reported back to test-takers in the form of a numerical score and a percentile rank. The goal is to rank the set of examinees so that decisions about their opportunity for success (e.g., college entrance) can be made. Standardized examinations such as SAT and TOEFL are typical examples of norm-referenced tests.

Criterion-referenced tests are designed to measure a test-taker's performance against a fixed set of predetermined criteria or learning standards (e.g., written descriptions of what students are expected to know and be able to do at a specific stage of their education). The primary goal of the tests is to determine whether or not test-takers mastered a certain skill or set of skills. In some cases, the results are "pass" or "fail" and are used in making decisions about job entry, certification, or licensure. In other words, criterion-referenced tests do not

262

aim to compare a learner to others, but they measure whether a learner reaches certain levels or achieves an instructional goal (e.g., achievement tests).

• Achievement Tests

An achievement test is the most commonly used type of test in the classroom. It evaluates students' understanding of a specific course or program. Achievement tests are designed with particular reference to the course objectives of a specific class and measure students' mastery of a particular instructional domain. In other words, the content of achievement is limited to particular materials which have been addressed within a particular time frame. For example, after finishing units 1 to 4 in a textbook, a teacher gives students an achievement test based on what they have studied in these units. Thus, achievement tests can also serve the diagnostic function in that they indicate the areas students need to work on in the future. However, the primary goal of the test is to determine whether students have met the course objectives by the end of a given period of instruction.

• Diagnostic Tests

The purpose of diagnostic tests in education is to assess the current state of a student's ability in a particular area to decide what needs to be taught or focused in the course. For instance, a test in pronunciation diagnoses the phonological features of English that are difficult to learners and the test results should be reflected in the curriculum. At the start of the writing course, the teacher gives learners a diagnostic writing test to see what areas of language need to be in the syllabus. The main difference between a diagnostic test and an achievement test is that the latter assesses the extent to which students have acquired language features that have already been taught throughout the course while the former aims to elicit information on what students need to work on in the future.

• Proficiency Tests

A proficiency test measures students' global competence in a language. Unlike achievement tests, a proficiency test is not limited to any one curriculum and specific materials. Rather, it tests overall ability. TOEFL and IELTS are examples of proficiency tests. They are almost always summative and norm-referenced. The tests play a role of "gate-keeping" since they are used to accept or deny "someone's passage into the next level of education" (Brown & Abeywickrama, 2010, p. 11). Since proficiency tests are uncommon within the classroom, they are usually developed by the institute for assessment. Proficiency tests often have a significant *backwash effect* on the classroom, as learners narrow their focus to the preparation of the test items.

264

• **Placement Tests**

The purpose of placement tests is to place students into a particular level of a language curriculum or school. Achievement tests and proficiency tests can be used as a placement test. In some cases, but not always, the test includes sample materials to be covered in the curriculum and it has some diagnostic features.

Principles of Assessment

A typical formal assessment is conducted in the form of a test. But, what is a good test? What are the criteria we can use to evaluate whether a test is good or not? Three classical criteria, reliability, validity, and practicality, need to be considered. This section will explain what these criteria mean in addition to two other important issues in language testing, authenticity and washback.

• **Reliability**

Reliability has to do with consistency. If a test is not reliable, we can find the source of unreliability from the test itself or the scoring of the test. The first case is called test reliability. For example, if you were to administer a test with high reliability to an examinee on two occasions, you would be very likely to reach the same conclusions about the examinee's performance both times. A test with poor reliability, however, might result in very different scores for the examinee across the two test administrations. The other source of the measure of reliability is a scorer, and this is called inter-rater reliability – the degree of agreement between two or more raters in their evaluations. For instance, a student's test is evaluated by two teachers, and one gives her an A, but the other teacher gives her a C. There is a big gap between the raters. The inter-rater reliability can be problematic when a test is open-ended and assessing students' oral or wiring performance, and it can be threatened when scoring directions are unclear and unspecific and when raters are not trained. Thus, the inter-rater reliability can be enhanced if judges receive clear and specific directions and guidelines as to the exact details they should attend to, and if they receive proper training to practice scoring. See the examples below:

Example 10.3: Oral Presentation Checklist

Evaluation of oral presentation

Assign a number to each box according to your assessment of the various aspects of the speaker's presentation.

3 Excellent

2 Good

1 Fair

0 Poor

Content:

□ The purpose of the presentation was accomplished.

□ The introduction was lively and got my attention.

□ The main idea or point was clearly stated from the beginning.

□ The supporting points were
  –clearly expressed
  –supported well by facts, argument
□ The conclusion restated the main idea or purpose.

Delivery:
□ The speaker used gestures and body language well.
□ The speaker maintained eye contact with the audience.
□ The speaker used notes (and did not read a script verbatim)
□ The speaker's language was natural and fluent.
□ The speaker's volume of speech was appropriate.
□ The speaker's rate of speech was appropriate.
□ The speaker's pronunciation was clear and comprehensible.
□ The speaker's grammar was correct and didn't prevent understanding.
□ The speaker used visual aids, handouts, etc., effectively.
□ The speaker showed enthusiasm and interest.
□ (If appropriate) The speaker responded to audience questions well.

(Adapted from Brown & Abeywickrama, 2010, p. 219)

Example 10.4: Written Language Assessment Activity (Years 8–10)

Explanation: An explanation is a factual text used to explain the processes involved in the evaluation of natural and social phenomena or how something works. Explanations are used to account for why things are as they are, focusing on causal relations. In the school curriculum, explanations are often found in Science and Social Studies.

Name of Student: ____________ Year Level/Class: ____
Topic of explanation: ________________

Criteria (Check appropriate column) Ability to carry out the task	Very competent	Competent	Limited not competent yet
Did the student – write an explanation with minimal support			
Structure and organization – introduce the issue/make a general statement – use logical, sequenced explanation of how/why something occurs – use paragraphs			
Language features – use appropriate subject vocabulary – use appropriate tense – use passive voice (optional) – use relevant linking words (e.g., if, when, because, consequently, since) – express relationships between concepts, particularly time and cause/effect relationships – use nominalized processes – develop themes logically that are consistent with explanation – use language to maintain appropriate tenor – support text with diagram (optional)			
Accuracy: – use grammar accurately, e.g., word order, verb endings, pronouns – spell and use punctuation accurately			
General Comments:			
General rating (circle) Lowest 1 2 3 4 5 Highest			

(Adapted from Nunan, 1999, p. 284)

268

Both of the above examples clearly point out which elements raters should pay attention to, what they evaluate in the oral presentation and the explanatory composition, and how they score. These clear guidelines help raters be as objective as possible and result in consistent evaluation across raters.

• Validity

Validity refers to whether or not the test measures what it claims to measure. A test with high validity consists of test items or questions that are closely related to the intended focus of the test. For instance, a valid reading test measures reading ability not previous knowledge of a specific subject. Certification and licensure tests with high validity include the items which are highly linked to a specific job or occupation. If a test is low in validity, it does not measure the job-related content and competencies it ought to. When this is the case, there is no justification for using the test results for their intended purpose. So, how can teachers somewhat assure that a test is valid? There are three ways to estimate the validity of a test: content validity, criteria validity (i.e., concurrent validity and predictive validity), and construct validity.

Content validity

In the classroom, the content validity refers to the extent to which the content of the test matches the instructional objectives. For example, a semester English examination should only include content covered during the semester, and it is not a valid measure of students' overall proficiency in English. As another example, let us assume that a school wants to hire an English teacher. A teacher who got the highest score in the test the school board designed was hired. However, he proves to be an extremely poor English teacher. After looking at the test, the school board begins to see what went wrong. The majority of the questions were about grammar, and it led the school to pick the most talented grammar teacher. However, the school needs an English teacher who can teach various English skills. The content validity of the test was poor and did not fully represent the construct of 'being a good English teacher.'

Criterion validity

Criterion validity is related to whether a test reflects a certain set of abilities. There are two types of criterion validity: concurrent validity and predictive validity. Concurrent validity is a measure of how well a particular test correlates with a previously validated measure. For instance, a school invented a test to measure students' listening proficiency. Students' scores are highly related to their TOEIC listening scores. In that case, the test the school created has high concurrent validity.

Predictive validity involves testing a group of subjects for a certain construct, and then comparing the results with others obtained at some point in the future. For example, a university made and administered an entrance examination to decide which students to accept in an attempt to find the brightest students. However, it turned out that the accepted students fell short of the school's expectations. In this case, the entrance exam has poor predictive validity. Most educational and employment tests are used to predict future performance, so

270

predictive validity is regarded as essential in these fields.

Construct validity

In order to understand what construct validity means, it is first necessary to understand what a construct is. A construct is quality, proficiency, ability, or skill that occurs in the human brain and is defined by established theories. For example, "English language proficiency" is a construct, and "Self-esteem" is a construct. Tests are operational definitions of such constructs in that they operationalize the entity that is being measured (Brown & Abeywickrama, 2010). Let's say that a school wants to examine students' communicative competence in English. The first thing to do is to define what communicative competence means. Based on well-established theories of communicative competence, the school operationalizes it as students' ability to speak English in socially appropriate manner. If the test items are well made to examine this skill, we can say that the test has high construct validity, but, if not, it is poor in construct validity.

• Practicality

We can call a test practical if a test (a) stays within budgetary limits, (b) can be completed by the test-taker within appropriate time constraints, (c) has clear direction for administration, (d) appropriately utilizes available human resources, (e) does not exceed available material resources, and (f) considers the time and effort involved for both design and scoring (Brown & Abeywickrama, 2010). For instance, if a test requires a personal interview with 1,000 students, but only a handful of examiners are available, the test is not practical. If a test requires students to use personal computers, but not all of the students have computers of their own, the test is considered impractical.

• Authenticity

Authenticity refers to "the degree of correspondence of the characteristics of a given language test task to the features of a target language task" (Bachman & Palmer, 1996). As the growing emphasis on communicative competence in second language learning, it has been suggested that tests should reflect the use of language in the real world (Spence-Brown, 2001). Leung and Lewkowicz (2006) notes that authentic test tasks should be made based on learners' needs and events they might encounter in real life. Thus, authentic test is considered "true assessment of performance" (Wiggins, 1998, p. 21), as opposed to traditional tests, such as entrance examinations with multiple choice, gap filling, and true or false questions. Brown and Abeywickrama (2010) points out that an authentic test includes language that is as natural as possible and has items that are contextualized rather than isolated, including meaningful, relevant, and interesting topics.

• Washback

The term washback has been used to refer to the way a test

affects teaching materials and classroom management (Hughes, 2003). Washback is generally perceived as being either negative (harmful) or positive (beneficial) (Messick, 1996). Negative washback takes place when a test is based on a narrow definition of language ability; thus, it constrains the teaching/learning context. For example, if students' writing skills are tested by multiple choice items, there will be great pressure to practice such items rather than to practice the skill of writing itself. In other words, instruction may focus too heavily on test preparation at the expense of other activities. Positive washback occurs when a testing procedure encourages 'good' teaching practice. Brown and Abeywickrama (2010) suggests that a test that provides positive washback offers learners a chance to adequately prepare for a test and gives them feedback that fosters their language development. In classroom-based assessment, one way to ensure positive washback is through instructional planning that links teaching and testing. By selecting a test that reflects instructional and program goals, a teacher can more closely align testing with instruction.

Alternative Assessment

Tests are most commonly used to assess learners' knowledge and performance; however, it does not mean that this is the only way. Tests are one of many possible types of assessment. Indeed, as educators and teachers became aware of drawbacks of standardized tests and acknowledged that tests were not enough to measure learners' ability, additional measures of student learning have been proposed and widely employed in the classroom. From among these, this section covers two of the most normally used assessment tools: portfolios and reflective journals.

• Portfolios

Portfolio assessment is a useful alternative evaluation tool used to document students learning processes and achievements. Genesee and Upshur (1996) explains that a portfolio is "a purposeful collection of students' work that demonstrates… their efforts, progress, and achievements in given areas" (p. 99). Participants in the portfolio assessment process (e.g., teachers, students, parents, and peers) should be aware of assessment criteria in advance. Depending on the type of portfolio, the contents may vary. Possible contents include writing samples that may vary in genre, content, and style (e.g., laboratory reports, journals, taped performances, recordings, art, research papers, projects, photos, interviews, conferences, tests, quizzes, observations, and reflections).

Portfolio assessment is not defined by a single procedure, nor is there a single best way to use portfolios. However, its characteristics and attributes can be described using the acronym CRADLE, Collecting, Reflecting, Assessing, Documenting, Linking, and Evaluating (Gottlieb, 1995, 2000). Portfolio is a collection of students' work, and students can select what to include. Reflective practice is done by self-evaluation and journals. This is a crucial component in portfolio assessment in that reflections allow students the time and space to analyze their achievement in relation to class standards, evaluate their final products, and determine growth as well as needs (Fernsten & Fernsten, 2005). This process eventually helps students take responsibility for their own learning. Teacher and student both participate in the role of assessment. Clear goals and explicit criteria for evaluation should be provided, and clear criteria for evaluation, including what must be included in the portfolio and rubrics for evaluation, are vital to successful portfolio assessment. Portfolio is a document which shows students' achievement. It also creates links "between student and teacher, parent, community, and peers; it is a tangible product, created with pride that identifies a student's uniqueness" (Brown & Abeywickrama, 2010, p. 131). Finally, it takes time and efforts to evaluate portfolios, but it is a rewarding process.

The benefits of portfolio assessment have been extolled by many researchers (Brown & Hudson, 1998; Genesee & Upshur, 1996; Lynch & Shaw, 2005). To begin with, portfolios allow the teacher to employ individualized ways of assessing students and evaluating multiple dimensions of language learning. They may also be used in conjunction with other types of required assessments, such as standardized or norm referenced tests. In addition, portfolios provide students with opportunities to reflect their learning and encourage them to consider what has been accomplished and what must be done to make improvements, and this eventually fosters responsibility and ownership of their own learning. Students can have tangible evidence of their own work. Portfolio assessment can also promote interaction between the teacher and students.

• Reflective Journals

A reflective journal is a log of students' ideas, personal thoughts and experiences, as well as reflections and insights they have in the learning process of a course. Reflective journals generally take two forms: structured journals and unstructured journals. In the case of structured journals, students are given a specific question, or set of guidelines. In contrast, in unstructured journals, students write their thoughts and feelings with minimal direction. However, both structured journals and unstructured journals are expected to include the following features: a student's personal perspective on an issue, synthesis and analysis of the issue, and the description of personal experiences and integration of them into the issue under study.

Many benefits can be derived from the implementation of learning journals in the language classroom. First, it generates active learning by allowing students to reflect on their own learning and to become independent thinkers. The process of self-reflection can also enhance the development of critical thinking skills. Writing reflective journals can bring out improvement in students' writing skills by expressing ideas, personal experiences, and opinions. It also helps teachers to gain a better understanding of how students think and feel about the course, and the learning progress of students throughout the course. In order to implement reflective journals successfully in the classroom, the teacher should provide clarity about expectations and assessment criteria. In addition to that, the teacher should try to make students understand the purpose and benefits of reflective journals at the very beginning, and explain and discuss the policies concerning privacy and confidentiality of information with students. Provision of timely feedback to students is also crucial for successful implementation of reflective journals as an alternative tool of assessment in the classroom.

Chapter Concluding Remarks

Assessing students' ability is one of the major roles teachers need to play in the classroom. It is essential for them to employ and conduct the rational and proper forms of assessment according to the purposes of evaluation. As the teaching approach has shifted, the ways of measuring students' knowledge and performance need to reflect such changes emphasizing learning processes and integrated skills. To this end, teachers need to make efforts to triangulate different types of assessments (e.g., using tests along with portfolios and observation). Teachers should remember that assessments are an integral part of the teaching-learning cycle. More specifically, assessments enable teachers to plan an effective lesson since they inform them what their students know and do not know and where they should focus in the next lesson. In addition, assessments can spur students to set goals for themselves and encourage their retention of information though the feedback from the teacher, peers, and self-evaluation. Also, students will be able to diagnose areas of strengths and areas needing further work through assessments.

GLOSSARY

accuracy: It involves the correct use of the target language (i.e., conforming to the language system itself).

acquisition: A term used specifically by Krashen to express naturalistic and implicit learning that results in learners having ability to spontaneously use L2. In other words, acquisition occurs without learners' awareness of learning something, and this is similar with the process of child L1 development. For Krashen, acquisition contrasts with 'learning' which results in explicit knowledge (See learning). Acquired knowledge is similar with implicit knowledge and procedural knowledge.

aptitude: It refers to learners' inherent abilities for language learning.

authentic language: The type of language that is used in real life by native speakers of the language, and it is not modified for L2 learner convenience.

automatic processing/automaticity: The ability to retrieve items from long-term memory during language processing

278

without any or with only a very small delay. Automaticity frees up the limited attentional capacity, which can then be allocated to other tasks.

baby talk (known as motherese, caretaker speech, or child-directed speech): Speakers who interact with young children modify their speech, through simplification, elaboration, repetition, slower production, etc.

backsliding: It is learners' temporary regression to a lower developmental stage although they have progressed to a higher stage.

backwash effect: It refers to the way a test affects teaching materials and classroom management. It is generally perceived as being either negative (harmful) or positive (beneficial) – also called washback effects.

behaviorism: A theory of learning. Behaviorism sees learning as involving conditioning or the development of a relationship between a stimulus and a response. Language learning is seen as habit formations.

bottom-up processing: A type of cognitive activity that involves learners in the process of recognizing and decoding the individual components of language in order to comprehend a sentence or utterance. Learners start with the basic units of language and combine them to make meaning.

coherence: It refers to the connection of ideas at the idea level.

cohesion: It means the connection of ideas at the sentence level.

communicative competence: The ability to interpret and enact appropriate social behaviors, and it entails the active participation of the learner in the production of the target language.

Communicative Language Teaching (CLT): CLT emphasizes the communication of meaning in interaction rather than the practice and manipulation of grammatical forms in isolation. It also underscores the functions and purposes a language serves in different communicative settings.

comprehensible input: This is an important concept to Krashen's monitor model of SLA. He claims that language acquisition precedes when learners are exposed to language that is just slightly beyond their current proficiency level. He calls this type of input comprehensible input 'i+1.' He further argues that if learners are exposed to language that is already known to them, no acquisition can take place.

Content-based Instruction (CBI): CBI is a type of meaning-focused instruction in which academic subjects (e.g., science and mathematics) are taught in the target language. The primary goal of CBI is the learning of academic content.

contrastive analysis hypothesis: The hypothesis that second language acquisition consists of a transfer of L1 habits to the L2. It was thought that L2 acquisition involved the gradual learning of the difference between the L1 and L2. The greater the differences between structures in the L1 and L2, the more difficult the acquisition of the target language was thought to be.

controlled processing: Controlled processing requires explicit and direct effort from learners. It takes place with language that is less familiar with the learner. Learning proceeds from controlled to automatic processing through practice. See also automatic processing.

conversation analysis (CA): A type of analysis that examines talk. It is concerned with how interactional participants use language to make sense of the interaction, focusing on turn taking, repairs, and so on.

corrective feedback: Corrective feedback occurs in response to learners' production errors. It provides negative evidence

280

to learners about what is not possible in the target language (also called negative feedback).

Critical Period Hypothesis (CPH): A biological concept referring to the idea that there is a specific moment for language acquisition. See also sensitive period.

declarative knowledge: A type of knowledge that requires conscious reflection and that can be verbalized. Declarative knowledge is similar to explicit knowledge and contrasts with procedural knowledge.

deductive learning: Learning explicit rules and applying the rules to other contexts.

developmental errors: This refers to the type of error learners make as they progress an L2. This contrasts with transfer errors, which are caused by L1 influence. An example of a developmental error occurs in the learning of the L2 English past tense. Learners are likely to overgeneralize the rule of the regular past verb '-ed' to the irregular verb (e.g., eated, comed). Learners commit this type of error regardless of their L1s. It is also called intralingual errors.

direct strategy: Language strategies involving using the language, including memory strategies, cognitive strategies, and compensation strategies. See also indirect strategies.

errors: A systematic divergence in the learner's second language production from the target language.

error analysis: The study of errors learners made in the production of L2.

explicit instruction: Language teaching that draws learner attention to language items and rules. Oftentimes, explicit instruction involves the overt presentation of rules of the L2.

explicit knowledge: Explicit knowledge is knowledge that is

consciously available to learners. Learners are often able to verbalize their knowledge.

explicit learning: Learning that occurs with awareness. Leaners are consciously aware of the L2 feature being learned.

extensive reading: It generally involves rapid reading of large quantities of materials or longer readings (e.g., whole books) for general understanding, with the focus generally on the meaning of what is being read than on the language. It is also called reading for pleasure.

fluency: It has to do with smoothness of language delivery.

foreigner talk: A type of language that is modified by native speakers to communicate with L2 learners. It has the similar characteristics with caretaker talk such as simpler structures and words, repetition, a lower speech rate, etc.

fossilization: When L2 learners' interlanguage permanently stops developing, it is said to fossilize. Some researchers prefer to call this phenomenon stabilization, instead of fossilization, since it is difficult to prove permanent discontinuity of learning.

genre: It is used to describe categories of written texts that have recognizable patterns, syntax, techniques, and/or conventions.

implicit instruction: Language teaching in which learners are not explicitly taught linguistic items. Learners' attention is not actively directed to specific language forms.

implicit knowledge: Implicit knowledge is knowledge of language that learners are not consciously aware of. Learners use implicit knowledge to produce language and to make grammaticality judgements, but they may not be able to explain what rules they have used. It is the type of knowledge that all L1 speakers have of their first language. It is sometimes known as procedural

282

knowledge. It contrasts with explicit knowledge.

implicit learning: Learning without awareness of what is being learned. For instance, when learners practice communicating in the target language, they learn grammatical aspects without awareness of learning grammar.

incidental learning: Learning that happens without the learner's intention to learn. For instance, learners are involved in a communicative activity in which they are discussing a specific topic. The primary intention is to practice communication, but they may notice some grammatical structures.

indirect strategy: Strategies that support language learning without using the language directly. These include metacognitive strategies, affective strategies, and social strategies. See also direct strategies.

inductive learning: Learners are exposed to language samples, and they induce the rules from the given examples.

input: A term used to describe the language data that are available to the learner, including all the visual and auditory language stimuli that surround the learner.

instrumental motivation: A type of motivation that is characterized by the learner's desire for some type of rewards or advantages from L2 learning (e.g., getting a good job and passing a graduate requirement). Instrumental motivation contrasts with integrative motivation. See also integrative motivation.

intake: Intake refers to the intermediary stage between input and acquisition. Intake is a part of input, which is internalized by the learner.

integrative motivation: A type of motivation characterized by a desire on the part of the learner to associate with the target language and culture in some way (e.g., having a close relationship with a speaker of the language).

intensive reading: Intensive reading is a teacher centered approach and its aim is to help students obtain detailed meaning from the text, to develop reading skills, and to enhance vocabulary and grammar knowledge.

interactional language: It is person-oriented and creating and/or maintaining social relationships and its important features are those of identifying with other people's concerns and being agreeable to the other people.

interference errors: A type of error that is caused by L1 influence (also called interlingual errors). This contrasts with developmental errors.

interlanguage: Learners' language system which has characteristics of their L1 and the target language. It is systematic and dynamic at the same time.

Interlingual errors: See interference errors.

interpersonal function: Interactional language is person-oriented and social-type talk. Its main purpose is creating and/or maintaining social relationships.

Intralingual errors: See developmental errors.

Language Acquisition Device (LAD): A metaphorical concept that refers to the part of brain that is programmed for language acquisition. This concept was introduced by Chomsky to argue against behaviorists' perspectives on language learning. Chomsky asserted that children do not receive enough input to construct all of the sentences they are able to create, and he believed that LAD leads to language acquisition despite of the lack of input. This term is less commonly used. UG is more commonly used to explain Chomsky's claim of language acquisition.

language related episode: See meta-talk.

learning: A term used specifically by Krashen to refer to explicit learning and memorization of L2 rules. This is a conscious process. According Krashen, learned knowledge has a very limited role in learners' spontaneous use of L2: the only role is to help learners monitor their production. Learned knowledge is similar with explicit knowledge and declarative knowledge.

logical problem of language acquisition: See poverty of the stimulus.

meaningful learning: Learning that involves the connections of new materials to the learner's existing knowledge or schema.

metalanguage: It refers to language used to talk about language such as grammar terminology.

meta-talk: It refers to talk about the language itself (also called language related episode).

mistakes: Nonsystematic errors that learners produce. Mistakes can be considered slips of the tongue.

negative evidence: Information about what is not possible to do linguistically in the target language (e.g., corrective feedback and explicit instruction).

negative transfer: This takes place when the learner's L1 knowledge interferes with learning the target language.

negotiating for (of) meaning: A term coined by Michael Long to describe the process that takes place when there is a communication breakdown between two or more interlocutors. Meaning can be negotiated through discourse moves such as clarification requests and confirmation checks.

noticing the gap: Learners discover the difference between their own interlanguage forms and the target language forms. One way to trigger noticing the gap is providing learners with corrective feedback when they commit errors.

other-regulation: Sociocultural theory argues that learners go from being other-regulated, meaning that they require assistance from other people or objects in order to complete a specific task, to self-regulated.

output: The language produced by learners (e.g., either oral or written form).

overgeneralization: The phenomenon in which learners apply a rule in contexts where it should not be used. For example, learners apply the regular past tense '-ed' to irregular verb (e.g., goed, eated).

parameters: Parameters are associated with syntactic theory, specifically Chomskyan theory and Universal Grammar. Parameters are particular variations on a type of syntactic feature (e.g., null subject parameter).

phonics approach: It supports a bottom-up approach and suggests that for readers to be successful they must be able to break a word down into its smallest parts, the individual sounds.

positive evidence: It consists of examples of what is possible in a language.

positive transfer: It occurs when the learner's L1 knowledge facilitates learning the target language.

poverty of the stimulus: Learners acquire the underlying rules of a language and can generate an infinite number of grammatical sentences when they are only exposed to a finite amount of input. This is one of the mysteries of language acquisition. This poverty of stimulus is one of the phenomena which led Chomsky to propose his theory of UG. This causes logical problem of language acquisition.

principles: A term from universal grammar that refers to the underlying structural properties of language contained in the human brain. These principles are abstract rules that apply to all languages.

private speech: A concept of sociocultural theory. It refers to language we use when we talk to ourselves (also called inner speech).

procedural knowledge: Knowledge of how to do something without having to think explicitly about it. This is the type of knowledge that L1 speakers have of their first language.

process-oriented approach: It concerns the process of how ideas are developed and formulated in writing.

product-oriented approach: It is a traditional approach to writing and focuses exclusively on correct grammar, composing practice, using the conventions of layout correctly (e.g., letters), and spelling.

pushed output: According to the output hypothesis, pushing learners to produce more accurate language than they have produced is beneficial for L2 learning. The utterances that learners produce in such a context is called pushed output.

recasts: Utterances that repeat a learner's incorrect utterance, making only the changes necessary to produce a correct utterance, without changing the meaning.

register: The style of language that is appropriate in a given context (e.g., the formality of language).

reliability: It has to do with the consistency. If a test is not reliable, we can find the source of unreliability from the test itself or the scoring of the test.

restructuring: Qualitative changes or reorganization of a learner's interlanguage system as a result of new learning.

rhetorical patterns: Ways of organizing information. Rhetoric refers to the way people use language to process information.

rote learning: Rote learning consists of relatively isolated concepts that are learned verbatim without integration into one's existing cognitive structure.

scaffolding: It refers to the help that a proficient language user (native-speakers or advanced learners) provides to a novice (less proficient language user).

scanning: A reading strategy where learners quickly look over a written text to find a specific piece of information.

schema theory: It is based on the concept that past experiences create mental agenda that helps people make sense of new experiences

schemata: A reader's background knowledge has a great influence on reading comprehension.

self-regulation: A concept in sociocultural theory that refers to the goal of the learning process. Sociocultural theory argues that learners go from being other-regulated to self-regulated, where they no longer require additional assistance.

sensitive period: A weak version of the critical period hypothesis.

skimming: A reading strategy where learners quickly look over a written text to get a general idea of its contents.

stabilization: See fossilization

target language: The language that is being studied by a learner.

think-aloud task: A type of research method in which learners verbalize their thoughts as they perform an activity.

top-down processing: A type of cognitive process in which learners draw on their general knowledge and world experiences in order to help them understand the language they encounter.

transactional function: Transactional language pertains messages focusing on content and carrying factual information.

transfer: It refers to the cross-linguistic influences in L2 learning.

It is viewed as the influence of L1 on the L2.

ultimate attainment: The L2 learner's end state, once L2 learning processes have ceased and the system has stabilized.

Universal Grammar (UG): A theory of first language acquisition proposed by Noam Chomsky. It proposes that human beings are born with an innate and genetic ability for language, and this does not account for learning other things. UG is a set of innate constraints on language that all human beings bring to the task of language acquisition. Included within UG are principles and parameters. Principles are constraints on language that are invariant and apply to all natural human languages. Parameters are particular variations on a type of syntactic feature.

U-shaped behavior: The acquisition of a linguistic structure go through three stages: early forms appear to be correct, followed by a period of incorrect forms, with a final stage of correct forms.

validity: It refers to whether or not the test measures what it claims to measure.

washback: It refers to the way a test affects teaching materials and classroom management. Washback is generally perceived as being either negative (harmful) or positive (beneficial).

whole language approach: It supports top-down approach of reading. Proponents of the whole language believe that language is a complete system of making meaning, with words functioning in relation to each other in context.

willingness to communicate: Learners' readiness to engage in L2 interaction.

Zone of Proximal Development (ZPD): The distance between what individuals can do on their own and what they can do with assistance from another individual.

BIBLIOGRAPHY

Abb, B., & Freebairn, I. (1991). Blueprint intermediate. London: Longman.

Allwright, R. (1988). Observation in the language classroom. London: Longman.

Anderson, A., & Lynch, T. (1988). Listening. Oxford: Oxford University Press.

Anderson, N. (2012). Reading instruction. In A. Burns & J. C. Richards (Eds.), The Cambridge guide to pedagogy and practice in second language teaching (pp. 218-225). Cambridge: Cambridge University Press.

Bachman, L., & Palmer, A. S. (1996). Language testing in practice. NY: Oxford University Press.

Bailey, K. M. (1996). The best-laid plans: Teachers' in-class decisions to depart from their lesson plans. In K. M. Bailey & D. Nunan (Eds.), Voices from the language classroom: Qualitative research in second language classrooms (pp. 15-40). New York: Cambridge University Press.

290

Bailey, K. M., & Savage, L. (1994). New ways in teaching speaking. Alexandrian, VA: TESOL.

Bialystok, E. (1997). The structure of age: In search of barriers to second language acquisition. Second Language Research, 13, 116-137.

Bialystok, E., & Hakuta, K. (1994). In other words: The science and psychology of second language acquisition. New York: Basic Books.

Bialystock, E., & Sharwood Smith, M. (1985). Interlanguage is not a state of mind: An evaluation of the construct for second language acquisition. Applied Linguistics, 6, 101-117.

Birdsong, D. (1999). Introduction: Whys and why nots of the critical period hypothesis for second language acquisition. In D. Birdsong (Ed.), Second language acquisition and the critical period hypothesis (pp. 1-22). Mahwah, NJ: Lawrence Erlbaum Associates.

Birdsong, D., & Molis, M. (2001). On the evidence for maturational constraints in second-language acquisition. Journal of Memory and Language, 44, 235-249.

Block, E. (1992). See how they read: Comprehension monitoring of L1 and L2 readers. TESOL Quarterly, 26, 319-343.

Bloom, L. (1991). Language development from two to three. Cambridge: Cambridge University Press.

Bohlke, D. (2014). Fluency-oriented secondlanguage teaching. In M. Celce-Murcia, D. Brinton, & M. A. Snow (Eds.), Teaching English as a second or foreign language (4th ed.)(pp. 121-135). Boston: National Geographic Learning.

Bongaerts, T. (1999). Ultimate attainment in L2 pronunciation: The case of very advanced late L2 learners. In D. Birdsong (Ed.), Second language acquisition and the critical period hypothesis (pp. 133-159). Mahwah, NJ: Lawrence Erlbaum Associates.

Brown, G. (1995). Speakers, listeners and communication. Cambridge: Cambridge University.

Brown, G., & Yule, G. (1983). Teaching the spoken language. Cambridge: Cambridge University Press.

Brown, G., Anderson, A., Shilcock, R., & Yule, G. (1984). Teaching talk: Strategies for production and assessment. Cambridge: Cambridge University Press.

Brown, H. D. (2007). Teaching by principles: An interactive approach to language pedagogy. NY: Pearson Longman.

Brown, H. D., & Abeywickrama, P. (2010). Language assessment: Principles and classroom practices. NY: Pearson Longman

Brown, J. D., & Hudson, T. (1998). The alternatives in language assessment. TESOL Quarterly, 32, 653-675.

Brown, P., & Levinson, S. (1978). Universals in language use: Politeness phenomena. In E. N. Goody (Ed.), Questions and politeness: Strategies in social interaction (pp. 56-311). Cambridge: Cambridge University.

Brown, R. (1973). A first language: The early stages. Cambridge, MA: Harvard University Press.

Brumfit, C. (1984). Communicative methodology in language teaching: The roles of fluency and accuracy. Cambridge: Cambridge University Press.

Burstall, C. (1975). Collaborative action research for English language teachers. Cambridge: Cambridge University.

Burt, M. K. (1975). Error analysis in the adult EFL classroom. TESOL Quarterly, 9, 53-63.

Bygate, M. (2001). Effects of task repetition on the structure and control of oral language. In M. Bygate, P. Skehan & M. Swain. Task-based learning: language teaching, learning and assessment (pp. 23-48). London: Longman.

Canale, M. (1982). Evaluating the coherence of studentwriting in L1 and L2. Paper presented at the annual TESOL

Convention, Honolulu, Hawaii.
Canale, M., & Swain, M. (1980). Theoretical bases of communicative approaches to second language teaching and testing. Applied Linguistics, 1, 1-47.
Candland, D. H. (1993). Feral children and clever animals. New York: Oxford University Press.
Cao, Y. (2011). Investigating situational willingness to communicate within second language classrooms from an ecological perspective. System, 39, 468-479.
Carrell, P., & Carson, J. (1997). Extensive and intensive reading in an EAP setting. English for specific purposes, 16, 47-60.
Carrell, P., & Connor, U. (1991). Reading and writing descriptive and persuasive texts. Modern Language Journal, 75, 314-324.
Carroll, J. (1981). Twenty-five years in foreign language aptitude. In K. Diller (Ed.), Individual differences and universals in language learning aptitude (pp. 83-118). Rowley, MA: Newbury House.
Celce-Murcia, M. (2014). An overview of language teaching methods and approaches. In M. Celce-Murcia, D. Brinton, & M. A. Snow (Eds.), Teaching English as a second or foreign language (4th ed.)(pp. 2-14). Boston: National Geographic Learning.
Chapelle, C., & Roberts, C. (1986). Ambiguity tolerance and field independence as predictors of proficiency in English as a second language. Language Learning, 36, 27-45.
Chaudron, C. (1988). Second language classrooms. Cambridge: Cambridge University Press.
Chomsky, N. (1959). Review of B. F. Skinner. Verbal Behavior, Language, 35, 26-58.
Chomsky, N. (1965). Aspects of the theory of syntax. Boston, MA: MIT Press.

293

Clarke, M., & Silberstein, S. (1977). Toward a realization of psycholinguistic principles in the ESL reading class. Language Learning, 27, 135-154.

Cook, V. (1997). Inside language. London: Edward Arnold.

Cook, V. (2003). Effects of the second language on the first. Clevedon, UK: Multilingual Matters.

Corder, S. P. (1967). The significance of learners' errors. International Rearview of Applied Linguistics, 5, 161-170.

Corder, S. P. (1969). An intermediate English practice book. Madras: Orient Longmans.

Curran, C. (1972). Counseling-learning: A whole person model for education. NY: Grune & Stratton.

Curtiss, S. (1977). Genie: A psycholinguistic study of a modern-day "wild child". New York: Academic Press.

Day, R., & Bamford, J. (1998). Extensive reading in the second language classroom. Cambridge: Cambridge University Press.

Dekeyser, R. (1998). Beyond focus on form: Cognitive perspectives on learning and practicing second language grammar. In C. Doughty & J. Williams (Eds.), Focus on form in classroom language acquisition (pp. 42-63). New York: Cambridge University Press.

DeKeyser, R. (2000). The robustness of critical period effects in second language acquisition. Studies in Second Language Acquisition, 22, 493-533.

DeKeyser, R. (2001). Automaticity and automatization. In P. Robinson (Ed.), Cognition and second language instruction (pp. 125-151). Cambridge: Cambridge University Press.

Dörnyei, Z. (1995). On the teachability of communication strategies. TESOL quarterly, 29(1), 55-85.

Dörnyei, Z. (2001a). Motivational strategies in the language

294

classroom. Cambridge: Cambridge University Press.

Dörnyei, Z. (2001b). Teaching and researching motivation. Harlow: Longman.

Dörnyei, Z. (2005). The psychology of the language learner: Individual differences in second language acquisition. Mahwah, NJ: Lawrence Erlbaum Associates.

Dörnyei, Z., & Csizér, K. (1998). Ten commandments for motivating language learners: Results of an empirical study. Language Teaching Research, 2, 203-229.

Dörnyei, Z., & Ottó, I. (1998).Motivation in action: A process model of L2 motivation.Working Papers in Applied Linguistics, 4, 43-69.

Doughty, C. (1991). Second language instruction does make a difference: Evidence from an empirical study of SL relativization. Studies in Second Language Acquisition, 13, 431-469.

Doughty, C., & Pica, T. (1986). "Information gap" tasks: Do they facilitate second language acquisition? TESOL Quarterly, 20, 305-325.

Duffy, G. (1993). Rethinking strategy instruction: Four teachers' development and their low achievers' understandings. The Elementary School Journal, 93(3), 231-247.

Dušková, L. (1984). Similarity – an aid or hindrance in foreign language learning? Folia Linguistics, 18, 103-115.

Edge, J., & Garton, S. (2009). From experience to knowledge in ELT. Oxford: Oxford University Press.

Ehrman, M. E. (1996). Understanding second language learning difficulties. Thousand Oaks, CA: Sage Publications.

Ellis, N. (1993). Rules and instances in foreign language learning: Interactions of explicit and implicit knowledge. European Journal of Cognitive Psychology, 5(3), 289-318.

Ellis, R. (2012). Language Teaching Research and Language

Pedagogy. Hoboken: Wiley-Blackwell.

Ellis, R., Loewen, S., & Erlam, R. (2006). Implicit and explicit corrective feedback and the acquisition of L2 grammar. Studies in Second Language Acquisition, 28, 339-368.

Færch, C., Haastrup, K., & Phillipson, R. (1984). Learner language and language learning. Clevedon, UK: Multilingual Matters.

Ferguson, C. (1971). Absence of copula and the notion of simplicity: A study of normal speech, baby talk, foreigner talk and pidgins. In D. Hymes (Ed.), Pidginization and creolizationof languages (pp. 141-150). Cambridge: Cambridge University Press.

Fernsten, L., & Fernsten, J. (2005). Portfolio assessment and reflection: Enhancing learning through effective practice. International and Multidisciplinary Perspectives, 6, 303-309

Ferris, D. (2010). Second language writing research and written corrective feedback in SLA: Intersections and practical applications. Studies in Second Language Acquisition, 32, 181-201.

Fries, C. C. (1945). Teaching and learning English as a foreign language. Ann Arbor, Michigan: University of Michigan Press

Gabrielatos, C. (2002). EFL Writing: Product and process. Retrieved June 10, 2016, from: http://www.gabrielatos.com/EFLWriting.htm

García Mayo, M. P. (2002). Interaction in advanced EFL pedagogy: A comparison of form-focused activities. Interactional Journal of Educational Research, 37, 323-341.

Gardner, R. C. (1985). Social psychology and second language learning: The role of attitudes and motivation. London: Edward Arnold.

Gass, S. (2003). Input and interaction. In C. Doughty & M. H. Long (Eds.), The handbook of second language acquisition (pp. 224-255). Oxford: Basil Blackwell.

Gass, S., & Mackey, A. (2006). Input, interaction and output: An overview. In K. Bardovi-Harlig & Z. Dörnyei (Eds.), AILA Review (pp. 3-17). Amsterdam: John Benjamins.

Gass, S., & Selinker, L. (2008). Second language acquisition: An introductory course. NY: Routledge.

Gass, S., Svetics, I., & Lemelin, S. (2003). Differential effects of attention. Language Learning, 53, 497-545.

Gass, S., & Varonis, E. (1989). Incorporated repairs in NNS discourse. In M. Eisentein (Ed.), Variation and second language acquisition (pp. 71-86). New York: Plenum.

Gass, S., & Varonis, E. (1994). Input, interaction and second language production. Studies in second language acquisition, 16, 283-302.

Genesee, F., & Upshur, J. A. (1996). Classroom-based evaluation in second language education. Cambridge, MA: Cambridge University Press.

Goh, C. (2007). Teaching speaking in the language classroom. Singapore: SEAMEO Regional Language Centre.

Goldschneider, J. M., & DeKeyser, R. (2001). Explaining the natural order of L2 morpheme acquisition in English: A meta-analysis of multiple determinants. Language Learning, 51, 1-50.

Goodman, K. (1967). Reading: A psycholinguistic guessing game. Journal of the reading specialist, 6, 126-135.

Gottlieb, M. (1995). Nurturing student learning through portfolios. TESOL Journal, 5, 12-14.

Gottlieb, M. (2000). Portfolio practices in elementary and secondary schools: Toward learner-directed assessment. In G. Ekbatani & H. Pierson (Eds.), Learner-directed assessment in ESL (pp. 89-104). Mahwah, NJ: Lawrence Erlbaum Associates.

Gregg, K. (1984). Krashen's monitor and Occam's razor. Applied Linguistics, 5, 79-100.

Hafiz, F. M., & Tudor, I. (1989). Extensive reading and the development of language skills. ELT Journal, 43, 4-13.

Halliday, M. A. K., & Hasan, R. (1976). Cohesion in English. London: Longman.

Han, Z-H. (2004). Fossilization in adult second language acquisition. Clevedon, UK: Multilingual Matters.

Harmer, J. (2011). How to teach writing. London: Pearson Longman.

Hedge, T. (2011). Teaching and learning in the language classroom. Oxford: Oxford University Press.

Hendrickson, J. M. (1980). The treatment of error in written work. Modern Language Journal, 64, 216-221.

Hoffman, M. L. (1986). Affect, cognition and motivation. In R. M. Sorrention& E. T. Higgins (Eds.), Handbook of motivation and cognition (pp. 244-280). NY: Guilford.

Hoffman, S. Q. (1997). Field dependence/independence in second language acquisition and implications for educators and instructional designers. Foreign Language Annals, 30, 222-234.

Horst, M. (2005). Learning L2 vocabulary through extensive reading: A measurement study. Canadian Modern Language Review, 61, 355-382.

Horwitz, E. K., Horwitz, M. B., & Cope, J. (1986). Foreign language classroom anxiety. Modern Language Journal, 70, 125-132.

Hughes, A. (2003). Testing for language teachers. Cambridge, MA: Cambridge University Press.

Hulstijn, J., & Laufer, B. (2001). Some empirical evidence for the involvement load hypothesis in vocabulary acquisition.

Language Learning, 51, 539-558.

Hymes, D. (1971). On communicative competence. Philadelphia: University of Pennsylvania Press.

Ioup, G., Boustagui, E., EI Tigi, M., & Moselle, M. (1994). Reexamining the critical period hypothesis: A case study of successful adult SLA in a naturalistic environment. Studies in Second Language Acquisition, 16, 73-98.

Ishihara, N., & Cohen, A. D. (2010). Teaching and learning pragmatics: Where language and culture meet. Harlow, England: Longman Pearson Education.

Jimenez, R., Garcia, G. E., & Pearson, D. (1995). Three children, two languages, and strategic reading: Case studies in bilingual/monolingual reading. American Educational Research Journal, 32(1), 67-97,

Johnson, J., & Newport, E. (1989). Critical period effects in second language learning: The influence of maturational state on the acquisition of ESL. Cognitive Psychology, 21, 60-99.

Johnson, J., & Newport, E. (1991). Critical period effects on universal properties of language: The status of subjacency in the acquisition of a second language. Cognition, 39, 215-258.

Keefe, J. W. (1979). Learning style: An overview. In J. W. Keefe (Ed.), Student learning styles: Diagnosing and prescribing programs (pp. 1-17). Reston, VA: National Association of Secondary School Principals.

Kellerman, E. (1987). Aspects of transferability in second language acquisition. Unpublished doctorial dissertation, Katholieke Universiteitte.

Kelly, G. (2000). How to teach pronunciation. London: Person Longman.

Kim, J. H. (2011). Learner interpretation of teacher corrective intention of feedback in EFL classrooms. English

299

Language & Literature Teaching, 17(1), 81-99.

Kim, J. H. (2016). The effects of different types of oral corrective feedback on the development of explicit/implicit L2 knowledge of English articles. English Teaching, 71(3), 53-77.

Kim, J. H., & Han, Z-H. (2007). Recasts in communicative EFL classes: Do teacher intent and learner interpretation overlap? In A. Mackey (Ed.), Conversational interaction in second language acquisition: A collection of empirical studies (pp. 269-297). Oxford: Oxford Press.

Krashen, S. (1982). Principles and practices in second language acquisition. London: Pergamon.

Krashen, S. (1983). The relationship between theory and practice. In R. Blair (Ed.) Innovative approaches to language teaching and language learning (pp. 15-30). New York: Newbury House.

Krashen, S. (1984). Writing: Research, theory and application. Oxford: Pergamon Institute of English.

Krashen, S. (1985). The input hypothesis: Issues and implications. New York: Longman.

Krashen, S. (2004). The power of reading: Insights from the research. Portsmouth, NH: Heinemann.

Kroll, B. (2001). The composition of a life in composition. In T. Silva & P. K. Matsuda (Eds.), On second language writing (pp. 1-16). Mahwah, NJ: Lawrence Erlbaum Associates.

Lantolf, J. P. (2000). Sociocultural theory and second language learning. Oxford: Oxford University Press.

Lantolf, J. P. (2005). Sociocultural and second language learning research: An exegesis. In E. Hinkel (Ed.), Handbook of research in second language teaching and learning (pp. 335-354). NY: Routledge.

Larsen-Freeman, D. (1997). Chaos/Complexity Science and Second

300

Language Acquisition. Applied Linguistics, 18, 141-165.

Larsen-Freeman, D. (2001). Teaching grammar. In M. Celce-Murcia (Ed.), Teaching English as a second or foreign language (3rd ed.)(pp. 251-285). MA: Heinle & Heinle.

Larsen-Freeman, D., & Anderson, M. (2011). Techniques and principles in language teaching. Oxford: Oxford University Press.

Lazaraton, A. (2002). Quantitative and qualitative approaches to discourse analysis. Annual Review of Applied Linguistics, 22, 32-51.

Lazaraton, A. (2014). Second language speaking. In M. Celce-Murcia, D. M. Brinton, & M. A. Snow (Eds.), Teaching English as a second or foreign language (4th ed.)(pp. 106-120). Boston, MA: National Geographic Learning.

Lee, J., & VanPatten, B. (2003). Making communicative language teaching happen. Boston: McGraw-Hill.

Lenneberg, E. (1967). Biological foundations of language. New York: John Wiley.

Leow, R. (1997). Attention, awareness, and foreign language behavior. Language Learning, 47, 467-505.

Leung, C., & Lewkowicz, J. (2006). Expanding horizons and unresolved conundrums: Language testing and assessment. TESOL Quarterly, 40, 211-234.

Li, S. (2010). The Effectiveness of Corrective Feedback in SLA: A Meta-Analysis. Language Learning, 60, 309-365.

Li, S. (2013). The interactions between the effects of implicit and explicit feedback and individual differences in language analytic ability and working memory. Modern Language Journal, 97, 634-654.

Lightbown, P. (1983). Exploring relationships between developmental and instructional sequences in L2 acquisition. In H. Seliger & M. H. Long (Eds.), Classroom oriented research in second language acquisition (pp. 217-243). Rowley, MA: Newbury House.

Lightbown, P. (1985). Great expectations: Second language acquisition research and classroom teaching. Applied Linguistics, 6, 173-189.

Lightbown, P. M., & Spada, N. (1990). Focus on form and corrective feedback in communicative language teaching: Effects on second language learning. Studies in Second Language Acquisition, 12, 429-448.

Lightbown, P. M., & Spada, N. (2006). How languages are learned. Oxford: Oxford University Press.

Loewen, S. (2015). Introduction to instructed second language acquisition. NY: Routledge.

Long, M. (1983). Linguistics and conversational adjustments to non-native speakers. Studies in second language acquisition, 5, 177-193.

Long, M. H. (1990). Maturational constraints on language development. Studies in Second Language Acquisition, 12, 251-285.

Long, M. H. (1991). Focus on form: A design feature in language teaching methodology. In K. de Bot, R. Ginsberg, & C. Kramsch (Eds.), Foreign language research in cross-cultural perspective (pp. 39-52). Amsterdam: John Benjamins.

Long, M. H. (1996). The role of the linguistic environment in second language acquisition. In W. Ritchie & T. Bhatia (Eds.), Handbooks of second language acquisition (pp. 413-468). San Diego, CA: Academic Press.

Long, M. (2003). Stabilization and fossilization in interlanguage development. In C. Doughty & M. H. Long (Eds.), The handbook of second language acquisition (pp. 487-535). Malden, MA: Blackwell.

302

Long, M. H. (2007). Problems in SLA. Mahwah, NJ: Lawrence Erlbaum Associates.

Loschky, L. (1994). Comprehensible input and second language acquisition: What is the relationship? Studies in Second Language Acquisition, 16, 303-323.

Lynch, B., & Shaw, P. (2005). Portfolios, power, and ethics. TESOL Quarterly, 39, 263-297.

Lynch, T. (1997). Nudge, nudge: teacher interventions in task-based learner talk. ELT Journal, 51, 317-325.

Lyster, R. (1998). Recasts, repetitions, and ambiguity in L2 classroom discourse. Studies in Second Language Acquisition, 20, 51-81.

Lyster, R., & Ranta, L. (1997). Corrective feedback and learner uptake: Negotiation of form in communicative classrooms. Studies in Second Language Acquisition, 19, 37-66.

Lyster, R., & Saito, K. (2010). Oral feedback in classroom SLA: A meta-analysis. Studies in Second Language Acquisition, 32, 265-302

MacIntyre, P., Burns, C., & Jessome, A. (2011). Ambivalence about communicating in a second language: A qualitative study of French immersion students' willingness to communicate. Modern Language Journal, 95, 81-96.

MacIntyre, P. D., Clément, R., Dörnyei, Z., & Noels, K. A. (1998). Conceptualizing willingness to communicate in a L2: A situational model of L2 confidence and affiliation. Modern Language Journal, 82, 545-562.

Mackey, A. (2012). Input, interaction and corrective feedback in L2 classrooms. Oxford: Oxford University Press.

Mackey, A., & Goo, J. (2007). Interaction research in SLA: A meta-analysis and research synthesis. In A. Mackey (Ed.), Conversational interaction in second language acquisition:

A series of empirical studies (pp. 407-452). Oxford: Oxford University Press.

Mackey, A., Gass, S., & McDonough, K. (2000). Learners' perceptions about feedback. Studies in Second Language Acquisition, 22, 471-497.

Masgoret, A. M., & Gardner, R. C. (2003). Attitudes, motivation, and second language learning: A meta-analysis of studies conducted by Gardner and associates. Language Learning, 53, 123-163.

Mayberry, R. I. (2007). When timing is everything: Age of first-language acquisition effects on second-language learning. Applied Psycholinguistics, 28, 537-549

Mayberry, R. I., & Lock, E. (2003). Age constraints on first versus second language acquisition: Evidence for linguistic plasticity and epigenesis. Brain and Language, 87, 369-384,

McLaughlin, B. (1987). Theories of second language learning. London: Edward Arnold.

McLaughlin, B. (1990). Restructuring. Applied Linguistics, 11, 113-128.

Messick, S. (1984). Assessment in context: Appraising student performance in relation to instructional quality. Educational Researchers, 13, 3-8.

Messick, S. (1996). Validity and washback in language testing. Language Testing, 13, 241-256.

Munro, M.,& Derwing, T. (2001). Modeling perceptions of the awareness and comprehensibility of L2 speech. Studies in Second Language Acquisition, 23, 451-468.

Murray, D. M. (1980). Writing as process: How writing finds its own meaning. In T. R. Donovan & B. W. McClelland (Eds.), Eight approaches to teaching composition (pp. 3-20). Urbana, IL: National Council of Teachers of

Education.

Murtagh, L. (1989). Reading in a second or foreign language: Models, processes, and pedagogy. Language, Culture, and Curriculum, 2, 91-105.

Nassaji, H., & Fotos, S. (2011). Teaching grammar in second language classrooms: Integrating form-focused instruction in communicative context. NY: Routledge.

Nation, P. (2002). Teaching ESL/EFL listening and speaking. NY: Routledge

Nation, P. (2003). Materials for teaching vocabulary. In B. Tomlinson (Ed.), Developing materials for language teaching (pp. 394–405). London: Continuum.

Neufeld, G. (1979). Towards a theory of language learning ability. Language Learning, 29, 227-241.

Newport, E. (1990). Maturational constraints on language learning. Cognitive Science, 14, 11-28.

Nicholas, H., Lightbown, P. M., & Spada, N. (2001). Recasts as feedback to language learners. Language Learning, 51, 719-758.

Nunan D. (1997). Listening in Language Learning. Cambridge: Cambridge University Press.

Nunan, D. (1999). Second language teaching and learning. Boston, MA: Heinle Cengage Learning.

Nunan, D. (2005). Task-based language teaching. Cambridge: Cambridge University Press.

Nuttall, C. (1996). Teaching reading skills in a foreign language. London: Heinemann Educational Books.

Nuttall, C. (2000). Teaching reading skills in a foreign language. London: Macmillan Education.

Ohta, A. S. (2001). Second language acquisition processes in the classroom: Learning Japanese. NY: Routledge.

Oller, J. W. (1979). Language tests at school: A pragmatics

approach. London: Longman.
O'Malley, J. M., & Chamont, A. (1990). Learning strategies in second language acquisition. Cambridge: Cambridge University Press.
Ortega, L. (2009). Understanding second language acquisition. NY: Routledge.
Oxford, R. (1990). Language learning strategies: What every teacher should know. New York: Newburry House.
Oxford, R. (1993). Style analysis survey (SAS). University of Alabama.
Oxford, R. (1999). Learning strategies. In B. Spolsky (Ed.), Concise encyclopedia of educational linguistics (pp. 518-522). Oxford: Elseviet.
Oxford, R. (2011). Strategies for learning a second or foreign language. Language Teaching, 44, 167-180.
Oyama, S. (1976). A sensitive period for the acquisition of a nonnative phonological system. Journal of Psycholinguistic Research, 5, 261-283.
Parker, K., & Chaudron, C. (1987). The effects of linguistic simplifications and elaborative modifications on L2 comprehension. University of Hawai'i working papers in English as a second language, 6, 107-133.
Patkowski, M. (1980). The sensitive period for the acquisition of syntax in a second language. Language Learning, 30, 449-472.
Pennington, M., & Richards, J. (1986). Pronunciation revisited. TESOL Quarterly, 20, 207-225.
Phillips, D. (2001). Longman complete course for the TOEFL test: Preparation for the computer and paper tests. London: Longman.
Raimes, A. (1998). Teaching writing. Annual Review of Applied Linguistics, 18, 142-167.

306

Ramsey, C. A., & Wright, E. N. (1974). Age and second language learning. The Journal of Social Psychology, 94, 115-121.

Reid, J. M. (1987). The learning style preferences of ESL students. TESOL Quarterly, 21, 87-111.

Reid, J., & Powers, J. (1993). Extending the benefits of small-group collaboration to the ESL writer. TESOL Journal, 2(4), 25-32.

Reinking, J. A., Hart, A. W., & von der Osten, R. (2002). Strategies for successful writing. Englewood Cliff, NJ: Prentice Hall.

Renandya, W., & Jacobs, G. (2002). Extensive reading: Why aren't we all doing it? In J. Richards & W. Renandya (Eds.), Methodology in language teaching: An anthology of current practice (pp. 295-302). Cambridge: Cambridge University Press.

Richards, J. C. (1998). Beyond training: Perspective on language teacher education. Cambridge: Cambridge University Press.

Richards, J. C. (2001). Curriculum Development in Language Teaching. Cambridge: Cambridge University Press.

Richards, J. C. (2008). Second Language Teacher Education Today. RELC Journal, 39(2), 158-177.

Richards, J., & Renandya, W. (2002). Methodology in language teaching: An anthology of current practice. Cambridge: Cambridge University Press.

Robinson, P. (2001). Individual differences, cognitive abilities, aptitude complexes and learning conditions in second language acquisition. Second Language Research, 17, 368-392.

Robinson, P. (2005). Cognitive complexity and task sequencing: Studies in a componential framework for second language task design. IRAL-International Review of Applied Linguistics in Language Teaching, 43(1), 1-32.

307

Rollinson, P. (2005). Using peer feedback in the ESL writing class. ELT Journal, 59, 23-30.

Rost, M. (1994). Introducing listening. London: Penguin.

Schachter, J. (1974). An error in error analysis. Language Learning, 24, 205-214.

Schmidt, R. (1990). The role of consciousness in second language learning. Applied Linguistics, 11, 129-158.

Schmidt, R. (1995). Consciousness and foreign language learning: A tutorial role on therole of attention and awareness in learning. In R. Schmidt (Ed.), Attention and awareness in foreign language learning (pp. 1-64). Honolulu: University of Hawai'i at Manoa, Second Language Teaching and Curriculum Center.

Schmidt, R. (2001). Attention. In P. Robinson (Ed.), Cognition and second language instruction (pp. 3-32). Cambridge: Cambridge University Press.

Schmidt, R., & Frota, S. (1986). Developing basic conversational ability in a second language: A case study of an adult learner of Portuguese. In R. Day (Ed.), Talking to learn: Conversation in second language acquisition (pp. 237-326). Rowley, MA: Newbury House.

Schwartz, B. (1993). On explicit and negative data effecting and affecting competence and linguistic behavior. Studies in Second Language Acquisition, 15, 147-163.

Segalowitz, N. (2003). Automaticity and second languages. In C. Doughty & M. H. Long (Eds.), The handbook of second language acquisition (pp. 382-408). Malden, MA: Blackwell.

Selinker, L. (1972). Interlanguage. International Review of Applied Linguistics, 10, 209-231.

Seow, A. (2008). The writing process and process writing. In J. Richards & W. Renandya, W. (Eds.), Methodology

308

language teaching: An anthology of current practice (pp. 315-320). Cambridge: Cambridge University Press.

Sharwood Smith, M. (1986). Comprehension versus acquisition: two ways of processing input. Applied Linguistics, 7, 239-256.

Sharwood Smith, M. (1991). Speaking to many minds: On the relevance of different types of language information for the L2 learner. Second Language Research, 7, 118-132.

Sharwood Smith, M. (1993). Input enhancement in instructed SLA: Theoretical bases. Studies in second language acquisition, 15, 165-179.

Sharwood Smith, M., & Kellerman, E. (1989). The interpretation of second language output. In H. W. Dechert & M. Raupach (Eds.), Transfer in language production (pp. 217-235). Norwood: Ablex.

Shin, D., & Nation, P. (2008). Beyond single words: The most frequent collocations in spoken English, ELT Journal 62(4), 339-348.

Skehan, P. (1989). Individual differences in second language learning. London: Edward Arnold.

Skehan, P. (1996). A framework for implementation of task-based instruction. Applied Linguistics, 17, 38-62.

Skehan, P. (1998). A cognitive approach to language learning. Oxford: Oxford University Press.

Spence-Brown, R. (2001). The eye of the beholder: Authenticity in an embedded assessment task. Language Teaching, 18, 463-481.

Stoller, F. L. (2002). Content-Based Second Language Instruction: What is it? Retrieved July 7, 2009, from http://www.carla.umn.edu/cobaltt/CBI.html

Stoller, F. L. (2004). Content-based instruction: Perspectives on curriculum planning. Annual Review of Applied

Linguistics, 24, 261-283.

Storch, N. (2005). Collaborative writing: Product, process, and students' reflections. Journal of Second Language Writing, 14, 153-173.

Swain, M. (1983). Bilingualism without tears. On Tesol, 82, 35-46.

Swain, M. (1985). Communicative competence: Some roles of comprehensible input and comprehensible output in its development. In S. Gass & C. Madden (Eds.), Input in second language acquisition (pp. 235-253). Rowley, MA: Newburry House.

Swain, M. (1996). Integrating language and content in immersion classrooms: Research perspectives. Canadian Modern Language Review, 4, 529-548.

Swain, M., & Lapkin, S. (1998). Interaction and secondlanguage learning: Two adolescent French immersion students working together. Modern Language Learning, 82, 320-337.

Swain, M., & Lapkin, S. (2002). Talking it through: Two French immersion learners' response to reformulation. International Journal of Educational Research, 37(3), 285-304.

Thornbury, S. (2005). How to teach speaking. London: Pearson.

Truscott, J. (1996). The case against grammar correction in L2 writing classes. Language Learning, 46, 327-369.

VanPatten, B. (1993). Grammar teaching for the acquisition of rich classroom. Foreign Language Annals, 26, 435-450.

VanPatten, B. (1996). Input processing and grammar instruction in second language acquisition. Norwood, NJ: Ablex.

Vygotsky, L. S. (1978). Mind in society: The development of higher psychological process. Cambridge, MA: Harvard University Press.

Vygotsky, L. S. (1986). Thought and language-revised edition.

310

Boston: MIT.

Vygotsky, L. S. (1987). Thinking and speech. In R. W. Rieber & A. S. Carton (Eds.), The Collected Works of L.S. Vygotsky. Volume 1: Problems of General Psychology (pp. 37-285). New York: Plenum Press.

Wallace, C. (1992). Reading. Oxford: Oxford University Press.

Wesche, M. (1981). Language aptitude measures in streaming, matching students with methods, and diagnosis of learning problems. In K. C. Diller (Ed.), Individual differences and universals in language learning aptitude (pp. 119-139). Rowley, MA: Newbury House.

White, L. (1989). Universal grammar and second language acquisition. Amsterdam: John Benjamins.

White, L. (1991). Adverb placement in second language acquisition: some effects of positive and negative evidence in the classroom. Second Language Research, 7, 133-161.

Wiggins, G. (1998). Educative assessment: Designing assessments to inform and improve student performance. SF: Jossey-Bass.

Williams, R. (1986). Top ten'principles for teaching reading. ELT Journal, 40, 42-45.

Wilson, J. (2010). How to teach listening. London: Pearson Longman.

Winitz, H. (1981). The comprehension approach to foreign language instruction. Rowley, MA: Newbury House Publishers.

Wode, H. (1981). Language-acquisitional universals: A united view of language acquisition. Annals of the New York Academy of Sciences, 379(1), 218-234.

Wong, J., & Warning, H. Z. (2010). Conversation analysis and second language pedagogy. NY: Routledge.

Yamaoka, T. (2005). From item learning to category learning: A learning process of procedural knowledge of learning. ARELE, 16, 21-30.

Zobl, H. (1980). The formal and developmental selectivity of L1 influence on L2 acquisition. Language Learning, 30, 43-57.

312